RADIOS

Wireless Sound

These and other books are included in the
Encyclopedia of Discovery and Invention series:

Airplanes	Movies
Anesthetics	Phonograph
Animation	Photography
Atoms	Plate Tectonics
Automobiles	Printing Press
Clocks	Radar
Computers	Radios
Genetics	Railroads
Germs	Ships
Gravity	Submarines
Guns	Telephones
Human Origins	Telescopes
Lasers	Television
Microscopes	Vaccines

RADIOS
Wireless Sound

by ROGER BARR

The ENCYCLOPEDIA of
D·I·S·C·O·V·E·R·Y
and INVENTION

P.O. Box 289011 SAN DIEGO, CA 92198-9011

Library of Congress Cataloging-in-Publication Data

Barr, Roger, 1951-
  Radios: wireless sound / by Roger Barr.

    p. cm.—(The Encyclopedia of discovery and invention)
  Includes bibliographical references and index.
    Summary: Traces the history of radio, from the discovery
  and harnessing of radio waves, to Marconi's development of
  the wireless, from the golden age of radio, to the present.
    ISBN 1-56006-225-8
    1. Radio—Juvenile literature.   [1. Radio—History.] I. Title.
  II. Series.
  TK6550.7.B295 1994
  621.384'09—dc20   93-12988
                                                    CIP
                                                    AC

Contents

Foreword

The belief in progress has been one of the dominant forces in Western Civilization from the Scientific Revolution of the seventeenth century to the present. Embodied in the idea of progress is the conviction that each generation will be better off than the one that preceded it. Eventually, all peoples will benefit from and share in this better world. R.R. Palmer, in his *History of the Modern World*, calls this belief in progress "a kind of nonreligious faith that the conditions of human life" will continually improve as time goes on.

For over a thousand years prior to the seventeenth century, science had progressed little. Inquiry was largely discouraged, and experimentation, almost nonexistent. As a result, science became regressive and discovery was ignored. Benjamin Farrington, a historian of science, characterized it this way: "Science had failed to become a real force in the life of society. Instead there had arisen a conception of science as a cycle of liberal studies for a privileged minority. Science ceased to be a means of transforming the conditions of life." In short, had this intellectual climate continued, humanity's future would have been little more than a clone of its past.

Fortunately, these circumstances were not destined to last. By the seventeenth and eighteenth centuries, Western society was undergoing radical and favorable changes. And the changes that occurred gave rise to the notion that progress was a real force urging civilization forward. Surpluses of consumer goods were replacing substandard living conditions in most of Western Europe. Rigid class systems were giving way to social mobility. In nations like France and the United States, the lofty principles of democracy and popular sovereignty were being painted in broad, gilded strokes over the fading canvases of monarchy and despotism.

But more significant than these social, economic, and political changes, the new age witnessed a rebirth of science. Centuries of scientific stagnation began crumbling before a spirit of scientific inquiry that spawned undreamed of technological advances. And it was the discoveries and inventions of scores of men and women that fueled these new technologies, dramatically increasing the ability of humankind to control nature—and, many believed, eventually to guide it.

It is a truism of science and technology that the results derived from observation and experimentation are not finalities. They are part of a process. Each discovery is but one piece in a continuum bridging past and present and heralding an extraordinary future. The heroic age of the Scientific Revolution was simply a start. It laid a foundation upon which succeeding generations of imaginative thinkers could build. It kindled the belief that progress is possible as long as there were gifted men and women who would respond to society's needs. When Antonie van Leeuwenhoek observed *Animalcules* (little animals) through his high-powered microscope in 1683, the discovery did not end there. Others followed who would call these "little animals" bacteria and, in time, recognize their role in the process of health and disease. Robert Koch, a German bacteriologist and winner of the Nobel Prize in Physiology and Medicine, was one of these men. Koch firmly established that bacteria are responsible for causing infectious diseases. He identified, among others, the causative organisms of anthrax and tuberculosis. Alexander Fleming, another Nobel Laureate, progressed still further in the quest to understand and control bacteria. In 1928, Fleming discovered penicillin, the antibiotic wonder drug. Penicillin, and the generations of antibiotics that succeeded it, have done more to prevent premature death than any other discovery in the history of humankind. And as civilization hastens toward the twenty-first century, most agree that the conquest of van Leeuwenhoek's "little animals" will continue.

The *Encyclopedia of Discovery and Invention* examines those discoveries and inventions that have had a sweeping impact on life and thought in the modern world. Each book explores the ideas that led to the invention or discovery, and, more importantly, how the world changed and continues to change because of it. The series also highlights the people behind the achievements—the unique men and women whose singular genius and rich imagination have altered the lives of everyone. Enhanced by photographs and clearly explained technical drawings, these books are comprehensive examinations of the building blocks of human progress.

RADIOS

Wireless Sound

RADIOS

Introduction

When English physicist Michael Faraday first suggested that electromagnetic waves, or radio waves, existed in 1832, he could not have foreseen how his observations would change the world. Since the first wireless telegrams were sent through the air on radio waves in the 1890s, radio has been the world's most important device for mass communication. The invention of voice radio in the early years of this century led to the birth of a new communication medium—broadcasting. Broadcast radio changed the country. People were greatly influenced by their favorite radio program, sometimes even to the point of changing their daily habits. The invisible walls that had separated America into distinct cultural regions began to tumble down. America became a more unified culture.

Today radio touches our lives in many other ways than broadcast radio and its visual cousin television—which uses radio waves to transmit its sound. Radio waves are used in many types of communication. Emergency vehicles,

... TIMELINE: RADIOS

1   2   3 4   5 6

1 ■ 1832
English scientist Michael Faraday suggests the existence of electromagnetic waves.

2 ■ 1864
James Clerk Maxwell, a Scottish physicist, proves mathematically that electromagnetic waves exist.

3 ■ 1887
German scientist Heinrich Hertz generates electromagnetic (radio) waves, verifying the work of Faraday and Maxwell.

4 ■ 1893
Nikola Tesla demonstrates an experimental wireless system in St. Louis, Missouri.

5 ■ 1901
Guglielmo Marconi receives the first transatlantic wireless signal.

6 ■ 1904
John Fleming invents the diode.

7 ■ 1906
Lee De Forest invents the triode; Reginald Aubrey Fessenden transmits the first voice radio message.

8 ■ 1912
Edwin Howard Armstrong develops the regeneration or feedback circuit.

9 ■ 1919
Edwin Howard Armstrong patents the superheterodyne radio receiver; Radio Corporation of America (RCA) is formed.

10 ■ 1920
Radio station KDKA in Pittsburgh, Pennsylvania, the first commercial government-licensed radio station, begins broadcasting on November 2.

taxi cabs, and delivery vehicles of all kinds depend on two-way radio communication to serve the public more efficiently. Long distance telephone calls of today seldom travel across the continent through wires. Instead, our conversations are turned into radio signals and relayed across the nation from tall towers or sent up into space to orbiting satellites and relayed to their destination.

Businesspeople use cellular radios to conduct business from their cars or carry pocket-size cellular radios to stay in touch with their offices.

With radio, we are reaching out to-ward the stars. Manned and unmanned spacecraft explore our solar system and radio streams of data back to scientists on earth. The stars themselves are reaching out to us, emitting radio waves that carry the secrets to the origins of the universe.

Remote-controlled radio waves even do little things for us, like opening garage doors at the push of a button. In its many forms radio has become a necessity in our lives.

11 ■ 1926
National Broadcasting Company (NBC), the first major radio network, is formed.

12 ■ 1933
Edwin Howard Armstrong receives five patents for frequency modulation (FM) broadcasting.

13 ■ 1939
The world's first FM radio station, W2XMN in Alpine, New Jersey, begins broadcasting.

14 ■ 1946
A radio signal is bounced off the moon and back.

15 ■ 1948
The transistor is invented by three Bell Laboratories engineers.

16 ■ 1954
The first portable transistor radio is marketed.

17 ■ 1961
Stereo FM broadcasting begins.

18 ■ 1962
Telstar, the first communications satellite, is launched into orbit by AT&T.

19 ■ 1981
Federal Communications Commission approves cellular radio service.

20 ■ 1992
Pocket-size cellular radio unit weighing less than one-half pound goes on the market.

Discovering and Harnessing Radio Waves

For centuries people have sought ways to communicate messages over distances without having to carry them by hand. Smoke signals, fires, flashing mirrors, ringing bells, and other methods have been used to send messages from one place to another. These methods were slow and often hampered by weather. They were effective only for limited distances over land. To communicate across great distances of land or water usually required messages to be carried by hand.

Slow communication sometimes led to tragedies that could have been avoided. For example, in the War of 1812 the United States and England reached a peace agreement in Ghent, Belgium, on December 24, 1814. Before word of the agreement arrived by ship in the United States, American and British troops had clashed on January 8, 1815, in the Battle of New Orleans. Faster communication could have saved the lives of more than fifteen hundred soldiers.

From the Known Toward the Unknown

The earliest discoveries relating to radio as a means of communicating over great distances seem far removed from the radio technology that we know today. The voices, music, and other sounds

The Battle of New Orleans, fought after the warring sides signed an agreement ending the War of 1812, claimed more than fifteen hundred lives. Faster communication, not yet possible, could have prevented these deaths.

Sir Isaac Newton discovered that visible light can be separated into seven bands of color. He called these bands a spectrum.

we hear on radio are carried on electromagnetic waves. The discovery of electromagnetic waves can be traced back to an important discovery about light that was made in 1671 by the great English scientist Sir Isaac Newton. Newton used prisms to separate visible light into seven bands of color. He called the bands a spectrum, a term derived from the word *specter*, meaning a ghostly figure.

Subsequent observations by other scientists added new bands, or waves to the spectrum. First, infrared or heat waves were discovered, followed by the discovery of invisible waves given off by the sun called ultraviolet rays.

Like most scientists of the early and mid-1800s, English scientist Michael Faraday knew of the existence of light and heat waves. He was also familiar with the mysterious properties of electricity and magnetism. For two centuries scientists had known of a relation-

ship between electricity and magnetism, but they had been unable to explain the nature of that relationship.

Faraday combined his own experiments with what he knew about light and heat waves, electricity, and magnetism. He proposed a theory that would unlock the door to the science of radio. In 1832 he suggested that the spectrum contained another form of invisible waves. Faraday called these waves "lines of force" and concluded that they were produced by the interaction of electricity and magnetism. Scientists today describe these waves as electromagnetic or radio waves.

Although Faraday could not prove the existence of these waves, proof was not far off. Thirty-two years after Faraday's dramatic announcement, a Scottish physicist named James Clerk Maxwell developed a series of mathematical equations that proved the exis-

James Clerk Maxwell developed a series of mathematical equations that proved the existence of electromagnetic waves.

ELECTROMAGNETIC WAVES

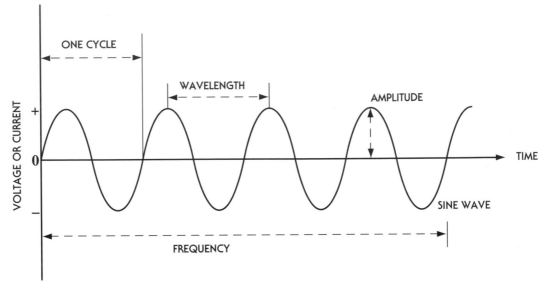

Mathematical equations developed by physicist James Clerk Maxwell demonstrated that electricity and magnetism travel in precise waves. Later scientists used this information to describe and measure electromagnetic waves. They found that electromagnetic waves move in a constant pattern known as a sine wave. Each repetition of the wave is known as a cycle. Within each cycle, the wave reaches a peak and a valley. The height of the peak (or depth of the valley) is known as the amplitude of the wave. The distance from the peak of one wave to the peak of the next is called the wavelength. The number of complete cycles within a certain period of time, such as a second, is identified as the frequency of the sine wave. These measurements allow scientists to compare and categorize electromagnetic waves.

tence of electromagnetic waves. Maxwell's equations, as they came to be known, demonstrated that electricity and magnetism travel in waves and that these waves move at the speed of visible light, 186,000 miles per second—a distance equal to seven times around the world.

Maxwell further assumed that electromagnetic waves traveled through an invisible, odorless substance in the air, which he called ether. Maxwell's ideas about ether were later proved false, but his equations proved to be an impor-

tant milestone in understanding the relationship between electricity and magnetism. From this beginning other scientists were able to describe electromagnetic waves in detail.

Producing Electromagnetic Waves

In 1887 a young German scientist named Heinrich Hertz performed a series of experiments that generated electromagnetic waves, confirming Faraday's theories of a half century earlier and proving the accuracy of Maxwell's mathematical equations.

Hertz fashioned an apparatus that had two metal balls separated by a narrow gap. He connected this device to a coil of wire, a battery, a switch, and a Leyden jar, a device that stored electricity.

When Hertz moved the switch to the on position, he completed an electrical circuit, which caused an electrical current to flow. An electrical current is the movement of tiny particles called electrons. It is a law of nature that electricity always flows from where there is a surplus of electrons to where there is a deficiency of electrons. Electricity that flows in only one direction is called direct current (DC). When Hertz first

Heinrich Hertz's simple experiments with electromagnetic waves laid the foundation for future radio technology.

turned on the switch, he started a direct current, but that was changed to alternating current (AC)—electricity that reverses rapidly its direction—by the Leyden jar and the coil of wire.

The alternating current caused a deficiency of electrons, known as a positive charge, to accumulate on one ball on the loop of wire and a surplus of electrons, known as a negative charge, to accumulate on the other ball. A spark jumped the gap from the negative ball to the positive ball, which neutralized, or canceled out, the charges.

When the direction of the current instantly reversed, the charges on the balls also reversed, and the spark appeared to jump in the opposite direction. In fact, however, it was still obeying nature by jumping from the negative ball toward the positive ball. Hertz called his device an oscillator because the spark oscillated, or switched back and forth, continuously, as long as the alternating current was maintained.

In further experimentation Hertz attached a metal ball to each end of a length of wire. He fashioned the wire into a loop but left a narrow gap at the ends. He then positioned the wire loop near, but not touching, the oscillator. When he turned the oscillator circuit on, a spark jumped across the gap in the loop. To Hertz this was remarkable. How, he wondered, could the oscillator circuit cause a spark to jump the gap in the loop when the oscillator and loop were not even connected? Hertz determined that the alternating current in the circuit had generated electromagnetic waves. These waves, he theorized, traveled through the air from the oscillator to the loop, igniting the spark that jumped the gap in the loop.

This simple experiment was the first

radio transmission. Hertz's oscillator circuit was the forerunner of all radio transmitters. The second loop of wire was the forerunner of all radio receivers.

The electromagnetic waves that Hertz had produced were called hertzian waves in his honor, a term that was later replaced by the terms *wireless* or *radio waves*. Hertz died just five years after conducting his ground-breaking experiments that became the foundation upon which radio technology would be built.

Early Wireless Technology

Hertz's successful generation of electromagnetic waves touched off a flurry of interest and experimentation among

Sir William Crookes showed uncanny foresight with his prediction that people would someday send and receive messages through the air without wires.

Bursts of electricity activate a pencil on Morse's telegraph. The pencil recorded dots and dashes along a moving paper ribbon.

scientists in many countries. In 1892 the English chemist Sir William Crookes, who also experimented with electricity, predicted that instruments for sending and receiving messages through the air without wires would be devised to make possible communication between persons in remote areas.

Scientists of the time described the instruments predicted by Crookes in terms of the electric telegraph, an 1840 invention by Samuel F.B. Morse. Morse's invention sent coded messages over wires strung between towns. The messages were transmitted using a coded system of dots and dashes or long and short sounds. This code, called Morse code, represented the letters of the alphabet. Sending messages in Morse code without the use of wires, therefore, was called wireless telegraphy.

The year after Crookes made his

HEINRICH HERTZ'S EXPERIMENT

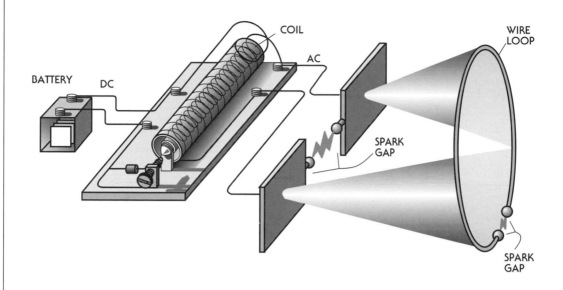

Heinrich Hertz was the first scientist to generate electromagnetic waves. He accomplished this while working with a device called an oscillator. The oscillator caused a current of electricity flowing through a circuit to reverse directions, causing a spark to jump back and forth across a small break in the circuit, known as a spark gap.

When Hertz threw the switch of the oscillator, a direct current (a current flowing in one direction) traveled from a battery through the wire coil and the Leyden jar. The coil and the Leyden jar changed the direct current into an alternating current (a current that quickly changes direction). The alternating current traveled through the wire to the spark gap. The current caused one side of the spark gap to build up electrons, creating a negative charge, while the other side lost electrons, creating a positive charge. When the build-up of electrons became great enough on the negative side, these tiny particles jumped across the spark gap. The movement of electrons through the air caused a brief, bright flash, or spark. Then, the alternating current changed direction and the electrons jumped the gap in the opposite direction. The sparking action continued as long as the alternating current flowed through the circuit.

Hertz added to his experiment by placing a loop of wire near the spark gap of his oscillator. Like the oscillator, the wire loop had a gap. When Hertz turned on his oscillator, he was amazed to see a spark jump the gap in the wire loop, even though the loop was in no way connected to the oscillator. Hertz reasoned that electromagnetic waves flowing from the spark gap of the oscillator had traveled through the air to the wire loop, causing the sparking. This was the first physical proof that electromagnetic waves existed.

prediction, a wireless system was demonstrated by the brilliant scientist Nikola Tesla. Tesla was born in the European country of Croatia in 1856 and immigrated to the United States as a young man. He worked with the great inventor Thomas Edison for a while but then set up his own scientific laboratory. In the 1880s Tesla designed and constructed the first electrical system that used alternating current. This system later became the standard for electrification in America.

After this success Tesla turned his attention to wireless telegraphy. In 1893 Tesla demonstrated an experimental AC wireless system in St. Louis, Missouri. His system was similar but superior to the oscillator and receiver built six years earlier by Hertz. In demonstrations Tesla's receiver was able to pick up waves emitted from the transmitter positioned thirty feet away.

Tesla also predicted that one day messages would be sent great distances without the use of wires. Tesla himself did little more to fulfill his own prophecy. Instead, he concentrated on other projects. When he did return to radio work years later, the technology had passed him by and his new research met with failure.

Research and experimentation on hertzian waves was continued by scientists in many countries. Some simply built their own versions of Hertz's apparatus and duplicated his experiments to witness for themselves the wonder of hertzian waves. Others made improvements on the equipment Hertz had developed.

The equipment that Hertz had used to detect electromagnetic waves was primitive and unreliable. The ability to detect waves easily was essential if a successful wireless communications system was to be developed. To make it easier to detect and eventually use electromagnetic waves, Edouard Branly of France developed a new device. It was later im-

Nikola Tesla devised a working wireless system that picked up waves emitted from a transmitter thirty feet away. His system was superior to any yet invented, but Tesla did not pursue it, moving on to other projects.

The Branly coherer (the tubelike device visible in the left-hand corner of an early wireless receiver) simplified the detection of electromagnetic waves. Detecting the waves was an important step toward learning how to use them.

proved by Sir Oliver Lodge of England. The device was a glass tube about the size of a thermometer, with a wire coming out of the tube at each end. The wires were attached to an electrical circuit. Inside the tube were metal filings. The tube replaced the wire receiving loop that Hertz had used, serving the same function as the gap in the loop. When an electromagnetic wave struck the tube, the metal filings stuck together, or cohered, completing an electrical circuit that rang a buzzer or bell.

As long as the tube was receiving the waves, the filings clung together, which kept the electrical circuit complete and made the buzzer sound. When the waves stopped, the buzzer

stopped, and the filings slowly separated. The device, which became known as the Branly coherer made the detection of electromagnetic waves much easier.

At this point scientists were still perfecting technology for detecting and sending hertzian waves. Although numerous scientists had recognized the commercial potential for sending messages using electromagnetic waves, none was able to construct a successful communications system. The field remained open for someone with a vision, someone who had the dedication to refine the existing technology and create a system that communicated messages without wires.

Marconi and Development of the Wireless

While some of the great scientific minds of the time were experimenting with wireless telegraphy, it was a young, self-taught man from Italy named Guglielmo Marconi who devised the first successful wireless telegraph system. Although Marconi's system used Morse code, it was such an important contribution to voice radio that some historians refer to Marconi as the father of radio.

Marconi was born into a wealthy family in 1874 in Bologna, Italy. He was a polite, quiet boy who preferred to spend time alone reading, rather than playing with other boys his age. In 1892, when Marconi was still in his teens, he read an obituary of Heinrich Hertz, the German scientist who had first generated electromagnetic waves five years earlier. The obituary described Hertz's equipment and his experiments. Like others, Marconi instantly recognized the commercial potential of the waves. If appropriate transmission and reception devices could be constructed, he believed that messages could be freed from the limitations of wire communications and go places where telegraph and telephone wires could not go.

Marconi set about the task of developing a commercial wireless system with an amazing dedication. He turned the third floor of the family home into a workshop and, fearing his work would be disrupted, forbade even the servants entry to clean. He read everything he could locate about hertzian waves.

Marconi refined the equipment that his predecessors had invented. Through trial and error he was soon able to generate hertzian waves with his equipment. But Marconi knew that merely duplicating the work of others was not enough if he were to develop a commercial wireless system. He started to make improvements in his transmitting and receiving equipment.

Because Marconi was untrained as a scientist, he achieved his results more

Guglielmo Marconi's tireless devotion to wireless technology led to his invention of the first successful wireless telegraph system.

through experimentation than reasoning. After countless experiments with his transmitter, for example, he replaced the Leyden jar with a better storage device called a capacitor. Marconi's transmitter included a copper plate behind the spark gap to help direct the waves toward the receiver. He also attached large copper plates to the sides of the spark gap. The plates stored the electricity generated by the current. When they were filled, they discharged, sending a large spark across the gap, which transmitted a powerful wave.

Further Research

After further experiments Marconi applied the same concept to his wave detector. He positioned similar copper plates near the coherer to increase its ability to detect waves. He then redesigned the coherer. After countless tests Marconi determined that filings made of 95 percent nickel and 5 percent silver stuck together the best. He ground the particles until they were as fine as dust. He narrowed the space in which the particles rested until a slip of paper would fill it. He extracted the air from the tube, which created a vacuum and eliminated interference from air particles. Marconi also added a device that tapped the coherer to loosen the filings once the electromagnetic waves had ceased. Each of these changes helped make the coherer more sensitive to the presence of electromagnetic waves and increased the speed with which these waves could be transmitted and received.

Marconi's work impressed many observers, including his father, Giuseppi Marconi. Originally, Marconi's father had not supported his young son's wireless research. However, as the elder Marconi saw the dedication of his son, he gave him one thousand dollars. With this money, Marconi was able to continue his research.

One of his ideas—attaching metal plates to each end of a tall pole and then burying one end in the ground—brought startling results. When Marconi transmitted a signal, the waves came across much stronger than they had before. Marconi also discovered that, by increasing the height of the pole, he also increased the distance the waves traveled.

By accident, Marconi had invented the grounded antenna, a device that became a staple in wireless and later radio communication. At the time he could not explain why this device made the waves stronger. The discovery illustrated a peculiarity about working in the new and invisible world of electromagnetic waves. Scientists often made discoveries without knowing why they worked. Sometimes it was years before they developed enough knowledge to explain why something worked.

These improvements allowed Marconi to transmit wireless signals to a receiver more than eighteen hundred yards away, farther than any other scientist had succeeded in doing. Further adjustments allowed him to transmit waves over hills.

Support for Wireless

Marconi, only twenty-two years old, approached the Italian government for financial support to continue his work. His request was politely but firmly refused. Disappointed but still deter-

Solving the problem of how to secure greater privacy for wireless users occupied much of Marconi's time.

mined, Marconi turned to his mother, who had originally come from England. The two journeyed to England. With his mother's help Marconi was able to secure an appointment with Sir William Preece, the chief engineer of the British Post Office. Preece had experimented with wireless technology himself. He was so impressed with Marconi's demonstration that he suspended his own work and became one of Marconi's biggest supporters. The successful demonstration secured additional financial support for Marconi to conduct further work.

By this time Marconi was sending wireless signals an incredible nine miles. Despite his success Marconi had

a serious problem to solve if he were to make his wireless system a commercial success. The telegraph and its new technological cousin the telephone, which sent voices over wires, were private media. Only those people on the transmitting and receiving ends could hear the message. But when the wireless transmitted waves into the air, anyone who had a receiver could pick them up.

Marconi had to devise a way to secure privacy. He knew that his transmitter sent the signals in all directions. He developed a set of reflectors that reduced the field of transmission from a full circle (360 degrees) to about 30 degrees. This limited but did not eliminate reception of wireless signals by others.

Members of the shipping industry followed Marconi's experiments with great interest. Communication between ships at sea and from ship to shore had always been difficult. The telegraph and telephone were of little use to ships because wires could not be extended out to sea. If it worked, Marconi's wireless had the potential to become an important communication device for ships.

Aware of the shipping industry's interest, Marconi moved his equipment to the Bristol Channel. On May 11, 1897, he began two days of futile tests in an effort to send signals across the channel. On May 13, he moved the coherer down to sea level. Although Marconi could not explain why, the result was a clear, strong signal. He later understood that the move had lengthened the receiver's antenna. This allowed the antenna to pick up more waves, which made the signal that was received stronger.

Marconi Enjoys Success

The Bristol Channel experiments caught the attention of the public. Marconi became an immediate celebrity in London social circles. In the United States *McClure's* magazine wrote extensively of Marconi's wireless experiments, generating interest in America. His success caused the Italian government to reverse its earlier decision and extend an invitation to Marconi to conduct further experiments in Italy.

In Italy Marconi discovered that wireless signals were blocked by the headlands, or steep hills that formed the shoreline. Again without understanding why, he discovered that by increasing the length of the transmission and receiving antennas, he decreased the problem. He eventually determined that the longer transmission antenna produced a longer wave that was less affected by hills.

Marconi knew, however, that there were limits to how big an antenna could be made. Improvements could not always be made through bigger equipment. Equipment had to be made *better.*

The Wireless Industry

While Marconi continued to experiment in Italy, Preece promoted Marconi's wireless system in England. His position in the British Post Office opened doors for Marconi that might otherwise have remained closed. Patents were secured for Marconi's equipment in both England and Italy. The patents issued by the two governments acknowledged that Marconi was the inventor of the equipment and therefore entitled to all of the profits derived from it.

Marconi returned to England and formed the Wireless Telegraph Company Ltd., which was later changed to Marconi's Wireless Telegraphy Company Ltd. to capitalize on Marconi's fame. He transferred his patents on the equipment to the company but retained control over them by owning a majority of the company's stock. The company would sell his wireless equipment, which could now send or receive messages for thirty-four miles. It would also send wireless messages for people who did not want to purchase their own equipment. This made Marconi a competitor of the telegraph companies.

On June 3, 1898, Marconi's company received its first income from sending five wireless messages. The total fee for the messages was a little more than one dollar.

Marconi had established himself as a tireless experimenter and a smart businessman. He now proved himself a great showman. In the summer of 1898 he chartered the tugboat *Flying Huntress* and reported the details of a yacht race off England's coast, sending more than seven hundred wireless messages to shore. Thanks to Marconi's wireless messages, newspapers had printed stories about the race before the yachts had returned to shore.

Marconi's success drew more attention for his wireless. He had proven the value of wireless signals to the press. Ship owners, impressed by Marconi's ability to send messages over water, began to purchase wireless systems and install them on their vessels.

Marconi conducted successful wire-less demonstrations for the marine insurer Lloyds, which strengthened the growing link between wireless and marine safety. As they approached the shore, ships equipped with Marconi's wireless system could signal the receiving stations that Marconi had erected up and down the coastline. Like lighthouses and fog horns, Marconi's wireless stations warned ships when they were approaching the shoreline. But the wireless could send signals from greater distances, and in all kinds of weather.

The value of wireless telegraphy to ships was demonstrated dramatically on March 3, 1899, when a steamer ran aground near a wireless-equipped ship stationed off the coast. The ship wired for help, and rescue crews rushed to the aid of the stricken steamer, saving both cargo and crew.

Marconi himself continued to pro-

Marconi and his associate, George Kemp, demonstrate the wireless telegraph in a scene from the first film ever made about this groundbreaking invention.

mote his wireless with carefully selected demonstrations. On March 27, 1899, he sent wireless signals across the English Channel to France. Although it did not cover a great distance, the demonstration established an important psychological link between England and the Continent. Marconi had always been quick to give credit to the inventors who had preceded him. With typical humility, Marconi's message on this occasion read: "Marconi sends his respectful compliments across the channel. This fine achievement being partly due to the remarkable researches of [Edouard] Branly."

A Visit to America

To promote the wireless in America Marconi journeyed to the United States the following September to report the America's Cup yacht races for the *New York Herald*. When the race was postponed because of poor weather, a rumor suddenly circulated that one of the yachts had gone down. The *Herald* wired Marconi out at sea. He immediately wired back that the boat was safe. Interest in Marconi's equipment boomed.

But Marconi faced competition in America. Other scientists were developing wireless systems, and some challenged his patents. He successfully defended a patent challenge from Nikola Tesla. Competition also came from a man named Lee De Forest.

De Forest was born August 26, 1873, in Alabama. As a boy he excelled in school and read constantly outside of his studies. At an early age he started to tinker with replicas and models of machines around him. De Forest kept a journal, recording his private thoughts

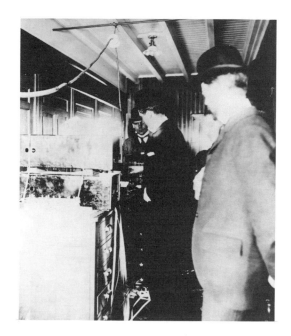

Marconi sends the first wireless marine message in America. Despite growing interest in his equipment, Marconi faced stiff competition from other inventors.

and dreams. As early as 1891 De Forest had written that he hoped to "become a rich and famous inventor" and to do good deeds with his money.

In 1893 he entered Yale University's Sheffield Scientific School in New Haven, Connecticut. There he attended a lecture by Nikola Tesla and soon concentrated his studies in the new field of electricity.

In 1900 De Forest patented a receiver that he called a responder. It consisted of two pieces of metal separated by a small space. After much experimentation he filled the space with a paste made of glycerin and lead peroxide, a substance he called "goo." The device worked better than Marconi's coherer because it was not necessary to tap the tube to dislodge the metal filings each time the circuit was broken. Marconi's system sent twelve words per minute, while De Forest's could send thirty-five.

Taking note of Marconi's use of yacht racing to promote his wireless, De Forest contracted with the Publisher's Press Association to cover the America's Cup yacht races in September 1901. Marconi was there with his own wireless to report the race for the *New York Herald* and the Associated Press. The race was postponed because of the assassination of President William McKinley. When it was held later, the two wireless systems interfered with, or jammed, each other, and the race had to be reported with traditional flag and hand signals.

The incident pointed out a continuing problem with wireless communication. The air was now becoming so crowded with wireless signals that they interfered with one another. A method to distinguish one message from another had to be developed.

In England Sir Oliver Lodge had patented a plan for regulating the wavelength of the transmitter and tuning the receiver to accept only that wavelength. Lodge determined that two properties, capacity and inductance, controlled the length of the wave.

Capacity, or the ability to store electric charge, is given to a circuit by the use of condensers. A condenser is made of two conductors of electricity that are separated by an insulating material. The larger the condenser, the more capacity it has.

Inductance is a property of an electrical circuit associated with electrical pressure or voltage. A varying electrical current in the circuit produces a vary-

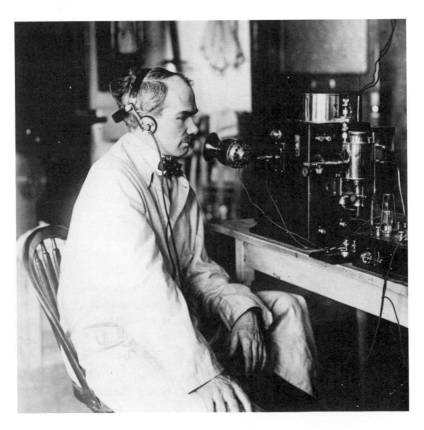

Lee De Forest dreamed of fame and fortune, both of which came to him through his work in the fledgling radio and electronics industries.

ing magnetic field. Together the current and magnetic field induce voltages in the same or another nearby circuit.

Inductance is given to the circuit by the use of an induction coil. Wrapping many turns of wire around a hollow cylinder created a coil. By varying the length of the coil, the receiver could be tuned to accept a specific wavelength and reject others.

Lodge determined that a transmitter and receiver must have the same capacity and inductance to work. He installed condensers of equal size on both the transmitter and receiver. The condensers tuned the transmitter to send waves of a certain frequency and also tuned the receiver to detect only waves of that frequency. Messages sent on other frequencies were not detected.

Marconi studied Lodge's work, then designed condensers whose capacity could be adjusted. He also designed adjustable coils. When the condensers and coils of both his transmitter and receiver were adjusted to the same size, they were tuned to accept the same wave frequency. Like Lodge's apparatus, Marconi's receiver detected only the desired message.

Marconi had patented his own tuning device in 1900 and later purchased Lodge's patent. He never used Lodge's patent, but owning it gave him a monopoly, or total control of the manufacturing of tuned wireless systems. Marconi's patents were unsuccessfully challenged in court by other inventors on both sides of the Atlantic.

By this time Marconi's company was the largest wireless company in the world. Ships outfitted with Marconi wireless systems regularly communicated with other ships and with stations on shore. Messages on land were sent over increasing distances from one Marconi station to another.

But Marconi wanted more. He dreamed of establishing a worldwide wireless communications network. To do that, Marconi knew that he would first have to establish a wireless link between America and Europe. At first he considered a plan to build stations on both sides of the ocean and transmit signals halfway across the ocean. That way, a ship traveling from Europe could switch to the American station at the halfway point (or the other way around) and remain in contact with land at all times. But Marconi knew that a direct wireless link between America and Europe was necessary for his worldwide network. He abandoned his original plan and set as his goal the transmission of messages clear across the Atlantic. Had his competitors known of his goal, they would have scoffed. No one had ever sent wireless signals over such great distances.

Spanning the Atlantic

During several visits to America Marconi had quietly laid the groundwork to start American Marconi. With companies on both sides of the Atlantic, Marconi could fulfill his goal to establish wireless communication across the Atlantic.

Marconi worked diligently toward his goal, traveling back and forth between Europe and America between 1900 and 1901. He built a station on Cape Cod, Massachusetts, and another at Poldhu on the western coast of England. A storm destroyed the Cape Cod station before any tests could begin. A new station was constructed in Newfoundland, Canada, the closest point on the North American continent to Europe.

Marconi spent the fall of 1901 preparing for his first transatlantic test. He experimented with various sizes of antennas. He increased the power of his transmitter so that it could hurl a signal across the ocean.

Finally, in December 1901, Marconi was ready. On December 10 Marconi and his assistants launched a kite that raised an antenna. The kite was an ingenious way to avoid constructing an antenna tower. However, Marconi was dissatisfied with the results. The next day he switched to a balloon, but the wind tore the balloon free, and he was forced to go back to the kite.

On December 12, 1901, Marconi again launched the antenna into a stormy sky using the kite. Marconi biographer Douglas Coe described what happened next:

> With deliberate movements [Marconi] lifted the telephone receiver and put it to his ear. The time had come.
>
> The other two [assistants] watched his intent but unreadable expression for several minutes. . . . And then Marconi turned to [assistant George Stevens] Kemp, holding out the receiver. "Can you hear anything?" he asked.
>
> Kemp flattened his hand against one ear to shut out the noise of the storm, and cradled the receiver against the other. And after a long moment he said, "Indeed I can. Distinctly."
>
> "Yes. I heard it too." Now Marconi allowed himself to smile.

History had been made. The men

Marconi demonstrates his wireless telegraph in 1902. By this time Marconi was hard at work establishing a wireless link between America and Europe. He viewed this as a first step toward a worldwide wireless communications network.

had heard the prearranged signal from England—three dots, Morse code for the letter *S*. The next day, after the signal was received again, Marconi announced to the world that he had spanned the Atlantic with wireless signals.

His news was greeted with skepticism. No one had ever sent a wireless signal that far, let alone over the ocean. The *New York Times* published a story about Marconi but carefully worded the achievement as Marconi's claim, rather than as fact.

The owners and operators of the transatlantic telegraph cables in Newfoundland, however, immediately recognized the significance of Marconi's announcement. They filed a lawsuit to stop Marconi, claiming they owned all the rights to the telegraph business in Newfoundland.

The lawsuit forced a delay in Marconi's attempts to open a transatlantic system. He put the delay to good use. A new station was constructed at Glace Bay in Canada. It included a new design for his antenna. It consisted of four wooden towers, each rising 210 feet into the air. Cables connected the tops of the towers, forming a giant square. Hundreds of wires attached to the cables were gathered directly over the transmitting building. The antenna looked like a giant wire funnel that would catch signals sent through the air from England and funnel them into the receiver.

The elaborate system did not function at first. Through trial and error, however, Marconi and his men found a way to make it work. When they disconnected three sides of the square, the antenna functioned better.

By now Marconi was under pressure from investors in his company to put the system into service. A year after the first signal had been received, Marconi conducted a demonstration for the *New York Times*. After several attempts a successful transatlantic message was communicated. The system was declared ready for service. But the system proved to be unreliable. Marconi knew that business considerations had forced him to hurry his system into operation before he was ready. He ordered it to be shut down.

A Reliable Link

Establishing a reliable wireless link between America and Europe proved to be an elusive goal for Marconi and the others who mounted their own attempts. The years slipped by as scientists worked to perfect their wireless systems.

While Marconi continued his research, Lee De Forest also improved his own wireless system. In 1904 De Forest exhibited his wireless system at the World's Fair in St. Louis. His demonstration was so successful that he received the grand prize for "general excellence in wireless telegraphy."

On March 28, 1906, a De Forest station on Coney Island in New York sent a thousand-word message to De Forest, who was in Ireland, more than three thousand miles away. Only about half of the message was received, but it was the most successful transatlantic wireless message ever sent. The event proved to be the highlight of De Forest's wireless career. By the end of that year bad management had forced his company to close.

For Marconi, five long years had

Marconi (seated at left) in the receiving room at his Glace Bay station in Canada. The station's newly designed antenna played an important role in the transmission of his first successful transatlantic message.

passed since his first wireless signal had spanned the Atlantic. Despite improvements to his equipment and countless tests, his goal of establishing reliable transatlantic wireless service still eluded him. On October 17, 1907, Marconi was finally ready for another public demonstration. Messages traveled back and forth across the ocean all day as his system worked perfectly. Marconi had finally achieved his goal.

Marconi went on to establish a vast wireless network that relied upon coded signals. Even as Marconi established this network, other scientists were experimenting with the wireless technology, developing communications systems that would carry not the dots and dashes of code, but the human voice and music.

CHAPTER 3

Voices Through the Air

On Christmas Eve in 1906 professional and amateur wireless operators in the area of Brant Rock, Massachusetts, sat at their receivers with their headsets covering their ears. Some had heard rumors that a special transmission would occur that night. At first they heard only the usual coded messages traveling back and forth through the air.

Then, from a small station in Brant Rock operated by Reginald Aubrey Fessenden came the coded message "CQ-CQ," a signal that information of importance to all stations was about to be

Reginald Aubrey Fessenden made history on Christmas Eve, 1906, when he sent voice and music over a wireless transmitter.

transmitted. What wireless operators heard next shocked them into momentary silence; then they called out to shipmates and family members in disbelief. For it was not the usual dots and dashes of Morse code coming into their headsets, but a man's voice! A woman's voice then rose in song, followed by the reading of a poem. Finally, a violin played the old Christmas hymn "O Holy Night."

At his station Fessenden laid down his violin and triumphantly listened as the wireless operators signaled each other up and down the coast in surprise and delight. "Did you hear that?" they signaled.

The voices and music had sounded strange and far away, but they were unmistakable. Unbelievable! How had this remarkable event come about?

Giving Voice to Wireless

As advanced as wireless transmitters and receivers had become, they were suited only to transmitting and receiving the dots and dashes of Morse code. The wireless signal transmitted by the spark-gap generator, a device commonly used for transmitting wireless signals, was a wave with a slow, steady frequency. Human voices and music create sound waves that rise and fall in modulation and frequency. Early attempts to transmit the irregular waves of voices and music with wireless technology resulted

Fessenden's Christmas Eve transmission was made possible by the invention of a new type of alternator designed by engineer Ernst Alexanderson. A later model Alexanderson alternator appears at left.

in transmissions where nothing came through at all, or only part of the signal was received.

In the early 1900s several developments occurred that allowed the sound waves of voices and music to be captured, transmitted, and received. The first development was the replacement of the spark-gap generator with a device that generated continuous waves that had a higher frequency. Working separately, two scientists developed different devices.

Valdemar Poulsen, a Danish scientist, observed that the flame created in an arc lamp pulsated as a continuous wave. With this concept he was able to develop a generator that produced continuous electromagnetic waves. Although the Poulsen generator was widely used, it never worked very well.

A more successful generator was developed under the guidance of Fessenden, an American scientist. Fessenden knew that the alternating current generator, or alternator, used to generate electricity to power lights and machin-

ery gave off electromagnetic waves. He also knew that higher frequency waves were necessary to carry voices. He believed that if he could develop an alternator that turned enough revolutions per minute to produce waves of 100,000 cycles per second, these waves would carry voices and music.

Fessenden worked with General Electric (GE), a company that built alternators. The first alternator built for Fessenden could not turn fast enough to produce waves of 100,000 cycles per second. A second machine was designed by a GE engineer named Ernst Alexanderson. This alternator had a stationary armature, or core, around which rotated a large tapered disc. The disc created an alternating current as it revolved around the armature's magnetic field.

Fessenden installed the alternator at his Brant Rock station in the fall of 1906. He was able to transmit voices in tests that fall. He chose Christmas Eve to make his first public transmission.

The waves that Fessenden sent into

the air that night were very different from wireless waves. The alternator generated a steady high-frequency wave called a carrier wave. To imprint his voice on that wave, Fessenden spoke into a device called a microphone. The microphone turned the sound waves of his voice into an electrical current called an audio signal. The irregular waves of his voice were then combined with the steady carrier wave into a new wave. This new wave had the rises and falls of Fessenden's voice and a high enough frequency to travel great distances through the air. This complex wave was transmitted and picked up by wireless operators. This transmission technique is called amplitude modulation, or AM because it modulates, or controls, the amplitude, or height, of the wave.

Fessenden's historic transmission signaled a shift in the philosophy of communication without wires. Wireless transmissions were usually intended for one recipient, yet no one had succeeded in devising equipment that made transmissions private. Fessenden's transmission, however, was intended for anyone who could hear it. He turned the disadvantage of the wireless's lack of privacy into an advantage.

The concept of sending a wireless message to a wide audience became known as broadcasting. The term *radio*, which created an image of waves radiating in all directions, began to replace the term *wireless*.

Using either the less reliable Poulsen generator or the Alexanderson alternator, many professional and amateur wireless operators were soon experimenting with sending voices through the air. Although the Alexanderson alternator was an improvement over the

Fessenden's wireless station in Brant Rock, Massachusetts. Fessenden's transmission, intended for anyone who could hear it, introduced the concept of broadcast radio to the world.

AMPLITUDE MODULATION

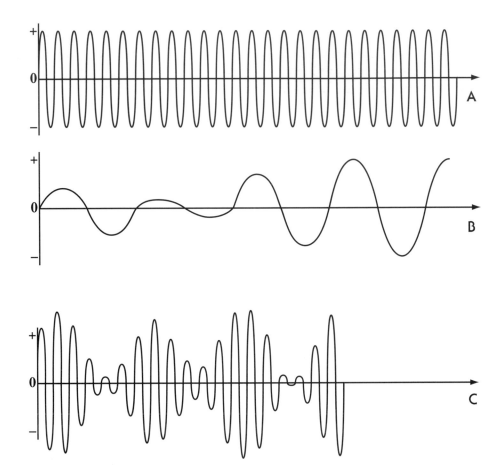

Amplitude modulation (AM) was the first method found to transmit sound via wireless signals. It combined a constant, high-frequency signal [A], known as a carrier wave, with an irregular signal [B] produced by a microphone. The result was a new kind of signal [C]. The frequency of this signal remained constant, but its amplitude varied as the signals from the microphone changed. Because the amplitude of the new signal changed, or modulated, it became known as amplitude modulation.

spark-gap generator, it had its disadvantages. It was a huge, mechanical device that was costly to build and maintain. It could be used only by stations that had a lot of money. A more compact, less expensive generator was needed.

Better transmitters were not the only requirement for voice transmission to be perfected. The wireless operators who heard Fessenden's Christmas Eve broadcast had done so with receivers designed to receive Morse code. The receivers lost part of the voice signal or reproduced it poorly.

Early radio engineers turned first to minerals called crystals. The molecules of crystals are configured in regular geometric patterns. It was discovered that a crystal changed the alternating current wave picked up by the antenna into a direct current by eliminating the negative pulses of the wave. The remaining portion of the wave duplicated the original sound wave generated by the voice or musical instrument. The volume of this wave was too low to be heard naturally. Operators heard the broadcast by attaching a set of headphones to the receiver.

Crystal receivers were inexpensive and popular among professional and amateur radio operators alike. However, they had one major limitation. The receiver operated on the low power generated by the received radio signal. This signal could not be amplified easily. Therefore, only an operator wearing headphones could hear a broadcast picked up by a crystal receiver.

A New Receiver

The key to developing better radio transmitters and receivers lay not in mechanical devices such as alternators or generators, but in the understanding and harnessing of the electron, the negatively charged particles that orbit the nucleus or center of an atom.

In 1904 Sir John Fleming, an English electrical engineer, developed a new receiver that surpassed the crystal and greatly advanced radio technology. Fleming based his work on experiments conducted in 1883 by America's most famous inventor, Thomas Edison.

Edison was working to perfect the electric light bulb. The light-producing element of his bulb was a carbon thread called a filament. When the electricity passed through the filament, it grew white hot and gave off light. Over time the bulb grew black, reducing its brightness. In an effort to eliminate the blackening, Edison constructed a bulb that had a small metal plate near the filament. He connected the plate to the positive pole of a battery and the filament to the negative pole. He believed that the positively charged plate would attract the black particles. Instead, a current flowed from the filament to the plate. When he reversed the battery connections, no current flowed. Edison noted the one-way flow of electricity which became known as the Edison effect, in his journals. He could think of no practical application for this discovery and went on to other projects.

Diodes and Triodes

It was not until the English scientist J.J. Thomson discovered the electron and its properties in 1897 that the Edison effect could be explained and put to use. The hot filament of the bulb gave off streams of electrons, which hovered around the filament. When the positively charged metal plate was brought near the filament, the negatively charged electrons flowed toward it.

When the charges on the plate and filament were reversed, the negatively charged plate repelled the negatively charged electrons, which were attracted by the positively charged filament. This effectively halted the flow of electrons and, thus, the flow of electricity.

In 1904 Fleming replaced the plate with a hollow metal cylinder that surrounded the filament. A battery heated the filament, but the plate was left unheated. Alternating current flowed into the bulb. The electrons flowed from the filament to the metal cylinder for half of the cycle. When the current reversed, so did the charges on the filament and plate. The flow of electrons stopped. Thus the device changed AC to DC, just as the crystal had done.

Fleming called his device a valve, because it turned the flow of electricity on and off, much like a valve governs the flow of water through a pipe. In the United States the device soon became known as a diode, which means two electrodes. Over time, as the glass outside became more tube shaped than bulb shaped, diodes and similarly con-

Lee De Forest holds an early version of his audion, later known as a triode. The triode was the first electronic amplifier.

structed devices were known as vacuum tubes, or simply tubes.

The invention of the diode was an important advance in radio technology. It used the power of the electron, rather than a mechanical device, to capture radio waves and convert them into direct current that was then changed to audio, or sound waves. The glass bulbs, however, were expensive to make, fragile, and bulky.

In 1906 Lee De Forest modified the diode to create a new device. De Forest had already patented some similar devices, but there is little evidence that they worked. In 1906 De Forest asked Henry W. McCandless, a manufacturer of automobile lamps, to construct a tube that included a filament and plate. Between them, and as close to the filament as possible, he installed a nickel wire. At the suggestion of John Grogan, one of McCandless's assistants, De Forest bent the wire in a zigzag fashion to create a larger surface to attract elec-

The Fleming valve, later called a diode, was an important advance in radio technology. It used the power of the electron, rather than a mechanical device, to convert AC to DC.

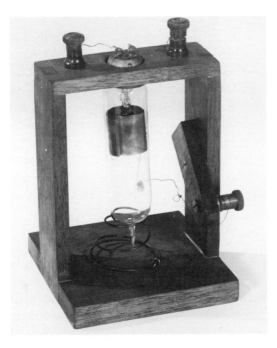

De Forest's triode, connected here to a radio receiver, paved the way for many innovations in electronics and radio.

trons flowing from the filament. He called this a grid.

The grid was positively charged. It attracted a stream of electrons from the filament and accelerated them toward the plate. The more positive the charge on the grid, the greater the charge on the plate circuit.

De Forest's device turned alternating current to direct current, just as the diode did, but it also amplified the audio signal received by the antenna, making it easier to hear. It was the first electronic amplifier.

De Forest called his device an audion, a combination of the words *audio* and *ion*. The very name he chose would later show that he did not understand how his invention worked. He mistakenly believed that the function of the tube was related to ionized, or charged, gases within it.

The triode, as De Forest's invention became known, was an important component in radio technology, and it became the founding invention for the wider science of electronics. For this reason, some historians call De Forest the true father of radio. Others contest this claim, saying that De Forest had borrowed heavily from the work of Fleming and Edison without acknowledging them—unlike Marconi, who readily acknowledged his predecessors.

In truth, many scientists made discoveries that contributed to the development of radio. No single individual can be credited with inventing radio. However, one American radio engineer stands out above all the rest. During a career that spanned nearly half a century, Edwin Howard Armstrong made some of the most important contributions to the development of modern radio.

Armstrong and Regeneration

Edwin Howard Armstrong was born in 1890 into a comfortable New York family. In 1904, when De Forest exhibited

TRIODE VACUUM TUBE

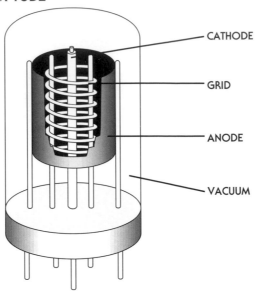

CATHODE

GRID

ANODE

VACUUM

The triode vacuum tube, invented in 1906, was the first electronic amplifier. It strengthened the audio signal received by a radio antenna, making it possible to hear weak radio signals more clearly.

The triode vacuum tube regulates the strength of radio signals received by the antenna. It does this by controlling the flow of electrons within a glass tube. The glass tube is drained of air, creating an airless chamber known as a vacuum. This is done because air can interfere with the flow of electrons. As an electric current flows through the tube, the cathode emits electrons. The anode collects these stray electrons. The grid, which is connected to the antenna, stands between the cathode and the anode. As the antenna responds to radio signals traveling through the air, it changes the charge of the grid. By assuming a more positive or a more negative charge, the grid controls the amount of electrons flowing from the cathode to the anode and, ultimately, to the speaker of the radio.

his wireless system at the St. Louis World's Fair, the thirteen-year-old Armstrong was already studying the experiments of Marconi and other pioneers that were written about in newspapers and magazines. Armstrong built his own wireless system and transmitted messages to others in the neighborhood. In 1908 he picked up signals from Key West, Florida, a remarkable two thousand miles away.

Armstrong entered Columbia University in New York in 1909 to study electrical engineering. In 1911 he set out to discover why De Forest's audion worked. A year later he concluded that the audion was a device that relayed electrons and that the current flowing from the plate in the tube oscillated, or moved back and forth, in a steady rhythm. He conceived the idea of feeding the oscillating current back into the grid to be amplified again. Since electrons move at the speed of light, he knew the current would be amplified thousands of times, greatly increasing the power of the signal received by the antenna.

This principle became known as feedback, or regeneration. The regeneration circuit became an important principle that is still basic to radio today.

Armstrong noticed in tests that when the radio signal reached its maximum amplification, the signal changed from a clear to a hissing sound. He decided that this was caused by the fact that the tube was not only receiving electromagnetic or radio signals, it was *generating* them as well. Armstrong's realization that his circuit generated electromagnetic waves was a turning point

Edwin Howard Armstrong's regeneration circuit could generate and receive electromagnetic waves. It replaced the bulky, mechanical generators and alternators used previously.

in radio history. At last the industry had found a replacement for the bulky, mechanical generators and alternators that had been used to generate high-frequency waves for voice radio. Engineers soon developed vacuum tubes that generated the high-frequency waves necessary to carry voices and other sounds. The huge, expensive generators were replaced by small, compact vacuum tubes.

Armstrong Versus De Forest

Although the young Armstrong was a brilliant radio engineer, he was naive regarding the business of radio. In filing his patent application for regeneration in 1913, Armstrong neglected to describe the oscillating features of his equipment. Had Armstrong been more descriptive in his application, it would have clearly established him as the inventor of regeneration. His oversight led to a long and bitter rivalry with Lee De Forest, the inventor of the triode. De Forest claimed that he had created regeneration in his own research.

There was more than honor at stake. Both men knew that whoever controlled the invention could make a fortune by granting licenses to companies that used regeneration in the radio equipment they manufactured.

For the next twenty years the two men battled in court for legal rights to regeneration. Eventually, the court ruled in De Forest's favor, and Armstrong was stripped of the title of inventor of regeneration. Despite the legal decision of the court, most members of the radio industry continued to recognize Armstrong as the rightful inventor of regeneration.

The diode, triode, and regeneration all made significant contributions to the advancement of voice radio. Yet voice radio was still in its very infancy. During the years that Fleming, De Forest, and Armstrong were at work in their laboratories giving voice to radio, wireless communication grew into an industry. Many events would combine in the next few years to turn wireless communication into voice radio.

CHAPTER 4

From Wireless to Radio

As the most visionary scientists dreamed of voices in the air, other scientists and businessmen were turning wireless telegraphy into a thriving industry. Around the globe wireless companies sprang up, and the world was united by invisible signals traveling through the air. With business interests in both the United States and Europe, the Marconi company remained the largest and most successful wireless company. Marconi himself remained the most famous radio engineer in the world.

Like all industries, wireless telegraphy had its share of get-rich-quick schemes. There were many business failures as con artists sold investors phony stock and then ran off with the money.

Even some of the most respected members of the industry were tainted with scandal. De Forest, for example, started several companies that sold his wireless systems, only to have them collapse because of fraud committed by his associates. Although De Forest himself was cleared of wrongdoing, one of his associates was actually sent to jail.

In 1912 a tragedy occurred that removed any doubt about the wireless industry's contribution to humankind. On the night of April 14 the *Titanic*, the largest, most luxurious ocean liner ever built, struck an iceberg on its first voyage. The collision ripped a three-hundred-foot gash in the liner's hull. Soon the crew realized that the impossible

The ill-fated Titanic *awaits its maiden voyage. Though it met a tragic end, the* Titanic *helped secure radio's place as an important communications tool.*

was happening. The unsinkable *Titanic* was going down on its maiden voyage.

The *Titanic*'s lifeboats were launched, but there were too few to save many of the *Titanic*'s passengers. The operator of the ship's Marconi wireless system tapped out a distress signal over and over. Less than ten miles away the liner *Californian* had slowed to a stop, surrounded by ice. The ship's one wireless operator had gone off duty, so the *Californian* never received the distress signal.

Forty minutes after the *Titanic* struck the iceberg, the liner *Carpathia*, nearly sixty miles distant, picked up the signal and responded to the distress call. The ship altered course and steamed toward the sinking liner at top speed. At 1:20 A.M., the *Titanic*'s distress signal disappeared. The *Carpathia* arrived in time to save 711 passengers, but 1,513 others perished in the icy waters of the North Atlantic.

The news of the *Titanic* disaster was transmitted around the globe by wireless. Marconi himself greeted the *Carpathia* a few days later when it docked in New York with the *Titanic* survivors aboard. The crowds cheered Marconi, whose wireless system had saved more than seven hundred lives.

There was a dark side to Marconi's achievement. Evidence later suggested that Marconi and others had manipulated the news surrounding the *Titanic* disaster. They withheld news, including the names of passengers lost, knowing that the prolonged suspense would hold the world's attention. In short, the disaster was good business for the growing wireless industry.

More importantly, the disaster pointed out the importance of wireless communication. More than seven hun-dred passengers owed their lives to wireless technology. Had the *Carpathia* not heard and responded to the *Titanic*'s distress call, many, if not all, of the survivors could have died.

But the disaster also pointed out grave inadequacies in the young industry. Had the *Californian*'s wireless system been staffed around the clock by an operator, the *Titanic*'s distress call could have been answered much faster, and many more lives might have been saved.

The disaster might have been avoided altogether had the *Titanic* heeded wireless reports of icebergs in the area and slowed its pace or stopped. Wireless had provided the *Titanic*'s crew with warnings that could not have been received a few years earlier, and the crew had ignored them.

As a result of the disaster, govern-

Although hundreds of Titanic *passengers died, others owed their lives to Marconi (below) and his wireless.*

ments entered the wireless industry, establishing regulations designed to prevent other tragedies. The wireless industry entered a period of more orderly development.

Big Business

More and more people saw the huge profits that could be made in manufacturing wireless equipment and establishing communications services. As a result, business rather than technological developments began to dominate the industry.

The wireless pioneers had labored away in their own laboratories, sometimes at great personal sacrifice, to create their inventions. Once an invention was patented, it could be marketed. Some, like De Forest and Marconi, founded their own companies to market their inventions. Other inventors sold their patents to companies. Fleming, for example, sold rights to his diode to the Marconi company, which used the device in its wireless systems. The age of the independent inventor was passing, replaced by large corporations that could finance the manufacture of wireless equipment. To get around the problem of purchasing patents, corporations created their own research laboratories and employed their own scientists.

Legal battles over patents sometimes hampered the technical development of the industry. One such suit was the battle between Lee De Forest and the Marconi company. Marconi owned the patent rights to the diode invented by John Fleming. In a lawsuit filed against De Forest, the Marconi company maintained that De Forest's addi-

tion of the grid to the diode was only a minor addition and that De Forest was violating the Fleming patent by manufacturing his audion. In a counter suit De Forest contended that the Marconi company had used his audion in its system without first obtaining his permission.

On the Marconi company's claim, the court ruled that De Forest's audion violated Fleming's patent. In an out-of-court settlement of De Forest's counter suit, the Marconi company admitted it had illegally used De Forest's audion. The effect of these conflicting proceedings was disastrous. Neither De Forest nor the Marconi company could use the audion without the other's permission. Since both sides sensed that huge profits were at stake, neither would grant permission. Consequently, for a time the audion could not be used by anyone.

Finding solutions to such legal problems became a daily headache for managers of wireless companies. With the exception of Marconi, few scientists had management skills equal to their skills as inventors. Marconi himself had become the idol of a young wireless operator named David Sarnoff. In the years ahead, Sarnoff would become a powerful figure in the industry, not as an inventor, but as a manager.

David Sarnoff

David Sarnoff was born in Russia in 1891 and came to America in 1900. He quickly learned English by reading the newspapers he delivered to help support his family. By the age of fifteen he had purchased his own newsstand. His entry into wireless telegraphy came

David Sarnoff, who once worked as Marconi's personal errand boy, predicted that the industry's future was in voice radio.

about by accident. He had entered the building that housed the *New York Herald* to look for a job. A wrong turn took him to a telegraph company, where he was offered a job delivering telegrams.

The job that Sarnoff had secured in 1906 was with American Marconi. He soon met Marconi and so impressed the great engineer that Marconi made Sarnoff his personal errand boy. By 1907 he had become a junior wireless operator, and a succession of positions followed. Sarnoff had been at the telegraph key of one of Marconi's land stations the night the *Titanic* sank.

Although Sarnoff understood the complicated technology that made wireless radio work, he knew that he was not an inventor. Like Marconi, he had the ability to see the industry as a whole and to identify trends. Sarnoff decided to concentrate on management.

Late in 1913 Sarnoff and a group of Marconi engineers watched a demonstration of Armstrong's regeneration circuit. Immediately, Sarnoff recognized that he had witnessed a demonstration that would one day revolutionize the industry. It would be several years before regeneration would find its way into radio equipment. But in that demonstration Sarnoff had gotten a glimpse of the future. He knew the future was not in the coded messages of wireless telegraphy, but in voice radio.

In 1916 Sarnoff drafted a lengthy memo to the head of American Marconi outlining what he perceived to be the industry's future. He believed that radio would become a household utility like the phonograph or piano. A transmitter would send signals to a receiver. Sarnoff wrote:

> The receiver can be designed in the form of a simple "Radio Music Box" and arranged for several different wavelengths (meaning several different stations), which should be changeable with the throwing of a single switch or pressing of a single button. . . . The box can be placed on a table in the parlor or living room, the switch set accordingly, and the music received.

Sarnoff foresaw the transmission of lectures, baseball games, and music from one part of the country to the other. Most importantly, he recognized that selling these radio boxes could mean large profits for the company.

Sarnoff was not the only one to envision a world in which radio was a part of every household. Lee De Forest had described a similar vision of radio's future in 1913, the same year that Sarnoff visited Armstrong's laboratory. However, the rest of the radio industry still perceived radio and wireless telegraphy only in terms of two-way communication. Sarnoff put his memo away, knowing that the industry was distracted by the war that had broken out in Europe.

Radio and World War I

War had erupted in Europe in 1914 between the Allies (Britain, France, Russia, Italy, and other countries) and the Central Powers (Germany and Austria-Hungary) after the assassination of Archduke Franz Ferdinand, heir to the Austro-Hungarian throne. Although the United States had remained officially neutral, many believed it was only a

The wireless radio industry had a profound influence on World War I. Field commanders used wireless communication to coordinate attack and defense plans.

matter of time before the country would be drawn into the war.

The war in Europe came at a time when the wireless industry in America was involved in a war of its own. Companies competed against each other for business. They battled in court for the patents that would allow them to control the industry.

When the United States entered the European war in 1917, the U.S. government declared a moratorium on the corporate and patent wars. It created a pool of patents from which all companies could draw. The government then awarded contracts to manufacture wireless equipment for the war effort to all companies as fairly as possible.

The wireless industry had a profound influence on warfare. Reports from the battlefront were sent by wireless radio to the rear, giving generals up-to-date information to determine troop movements. Field commanders used wireless communication to coordinate attack and defense plans. Using reports supplied by airplanes carrying wireless equipment, artillery gunners could point their guns with better accuracy.

Wireless radio introduced a whole new field of spying. The public nature of such communication allowed either side to listen to the other's transmissions. Stealing or breaking the code of the enemy became a common practice. Even if the code could not be broken, the transmission itself gave away the enemy's presence.

The war also had a significant effect on the radio industry. The moratorium on corporate competition brought together radio engineers who had competed against one another. Instead of competing, they were all working to-ward improving radio for the common goal of defeating the enemy. Previously companies had manufactured radio parts in small quantities. But the U.S. army and navy needed thousands of radio systems. The tremendous need forced the industry to mass produce its components. The war also helped introduce standardization to radio systems so that sailors and soldiers could operate any of them without having to learn how to operate a new system. As a result, the radio equipment produced at the end of the war was superior to what existed before the war began.

Armstrong and the Superheterodyne

There was one revolutionary development in radio technology whose roots were tied to the war. While serving in France in World War I, Edwin Howard Armstrong continued his radio research, concentrating on high-frequency radio waves.

Early in the century, Reginald Aubrey Fessenden had observed that when two notes of different frequencies were played together on a piano, they produced a third sound wave of a lower frequency. He coined the term *heterodyne* to describe this event, combining the Greek words *hetero* (other) and *dyne* (force). Fessenden had sought to apply this concept to high-frequency radio waves, but the technology of the time was too primitive.

Armstrong visualized a radio receiver that combined Fessenden's ideas with his own regeneration circuit. He called it a superheterodyne. The receiver would work in four stages. First, the receiver would pick up an incoming

SUPERHETERODYNE

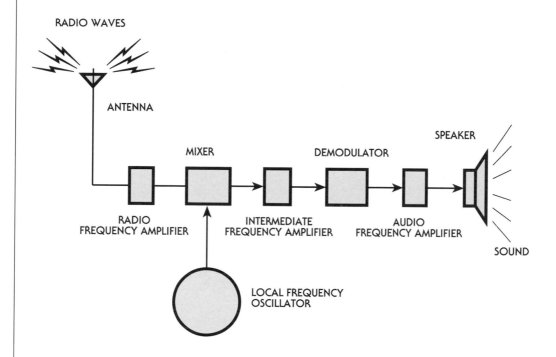

RADIO WAVES

ANTENNA

SPEAKER

MIXER

DEMODULATOR

RADIO
FREQUENCY AMPLIFIER

INTERMEDIATE
FREQUENCY AMPLIFIER

AUDIO
FREQUENCY AMPLIFIER

SOUND

LOCAL FREQUENCY
OSCILLATOR

Edwin Howard Armstrong's super-heterodyne is considered the first modern radio receiver. It improved radio reception by narrowing the frequency range handled by the amplifiers. This helped eliminate unwanted electrical interference while still boosting the radio signal. The superheterodyne has had a lasting effect on the radio industry. Almost all modern AM and FM receivers are superheterodynes.

In a simple AM superheterodyne receiver the antenna feeds electromagnetic waves striking it to the radio frequency amplifier. This amplifier screens out unwanted signals and strengthens signals from the desired station. The strengthened signals are then fed to a mixer. The mixer combines, or beats, the strengthened signals with signals produced by a local oscillator. Because each set of signals has a different frequency, a new wave frequency emerges from the mixer. The new waves are called intermediate, or beat, waves.

The intermediate frequency amplifier boosts the beat waves, resulting in a powerful signal. This signal then passes through a demodulator. The demodulator separates the audio signal from its carrier. The audio signal then passes through an audio frequency amplifier. This amplifier strengthens the audio signal and then feeds it to the speaker, which converts the signal into sound.

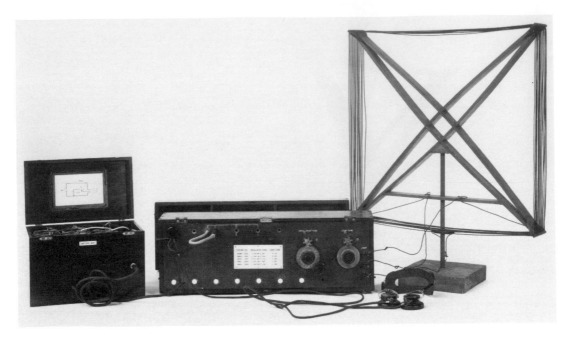

The influence of the early superheterodyne (above) is still strong today. Nearly all modern AM and FM radio receivers are superheterodynes.

radio wave of high frequency and combine it with another wave produced by a vacuum tube. The result would be a third wave known as the beat wave. Second, the beat wave would travel through an amplifier to increase its power thousands of times. Third, the regeneration circuit would detect that wave and turn it into direct current. Finally, the direct current would pass through another amplifier, which would convert it to sound waves that could be heard in earphones or over a speaker. Throughout this complex process the original sound and all of its modulations were kept exactly as they had been.

The superheterodyne had one other benefit. Although its circuits were the most complex of any receiver ever built, it was simple to operate. There was one knob that controlled the volume and one that changed the frequency to which the receiver was tuned. It was the first modern radio receiver, the prototype of all radio receivers we know today.

The war ended in 1918. Armstrong had completed enough work on his superheterodyne to apply for patents in France at the end of 1918, before he returned to America. In February 1919 Armstrong applied for a U.S. patent. The application was one of the most important in the industry's history. An entire industry would be built around Armstrong's invention.

Radio Comes of Age

World War I had begun just as voice radio was being perfected, and industry leaders were viewing radio as a broadcast medium, as well as a method of two-way communication. With the war over, everyone turned their attention toward business in America once again. But the war's legacy would greatly influence the development of the industry during the next decade.

Besides vastly improving radio technology, the war had altered the face of the emerging industry. In fulfilling government radio contracts, manufacturers of radio equipment had become aware of the large profits the industry offered. They were eager to carve out their own niches in the expanding market for communications networks and the sale of radio equipment. The corporate wars that had been halted by the government broke out again, more bitter than ever.

World War I had also fostered a new attitude about radio within the federal government itself. By creating the pool of patents during the war, the government had controlled the radio industry as well. Government officials understood how important radio had become, and they were not eager to see control of the new industry fall out of American hands, as the international telegraph industry had decades earlier.

When General Electric (GE) arranged to sell a number of the powerful Alexanderson alternators it manufactured to American Marconi, the U.S. government pressured GE not to go through with the sale. Because American Marconi was owned by British Marconi, the U.S. government believed the sale of the alternators went against the national interest.

Given the U.S. government's attitude, American Marconi officials understood that there was little future for the company in the United States. At the same time, GE officials wanted to expand into the radio business and sought to avoid the expense of competing directly against American Marconi.

The answer to both problems was the creation of a new radio company.

The radio industry blossomed after World War I, leading to the birth of broadcasting and home radio use.

HOW A RADIO BROADCAST IS CARRIED TO YOUR HOME

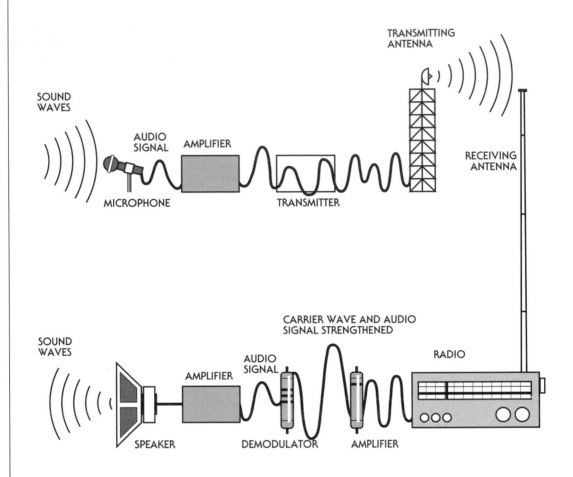

In a radio studio, sounds such as a voice or music enter a microphone. The microphone transforms the sound waves into a changing, or variable, audio signal. An amplifier strengthens the signal and sends it to a transmitter. The transmitter emits a carrier wave, which combines with the audio signal to create a modulated signal. The transmitting antenna sends the modulated signal through the air. The signal that reaches the receiving antenna of a radio travels through the radio's circuitry to an amplifier, which boosts the signal thousands of times. The strengthened signal proceeds to a demodulator, which separates the audio signal from the carrier wave. The audio signal then travels to an amplifier. The amplified audio signal travels to the speaker and causes it to vibrate. The vibration of the speaker creates sound waves that can be heard by the ear.

On October 17, 1919, the Radio Corporation of America (RCA) was formed. With General Electric serving as the parent company, the American Marconi company's assets and patents were transferred to the new company. The government, satisfied that RCA would always be owned by Americans, also transferred radio patents held by the U.S. Navy to the new company. Most of the Marconi employees became RCA employees, including David Sarnoff, who became commercial manager. During the next decade Sarnoff's influence within the new company would grow, and he would help turn RCA into the most powerful force in the American radio industry.

The spare surroundings of an early RCA broadcast studio belie the company's powerful influence on the American radio industry.

RCA Versus AT&T

In the scramble for business it soon became obvious that what happened in the courtrooms and corporate meeting rooms would influence the growth of the industry as much as would new scientific developments in the laboratories. Companies seeking to manufacture radio equipment often found the path blocked by the legal tangles of patent ownership.

The most important patent struggle was between RCA and American Telephone and Telegraph (AT&T). RCA had inherited the rights to Fleming's diode from American Marconi. AT&T, in the meantime, had secured the rights to De Forest's audion. The best radios could be made by combining the two technologies into a single radio tube. But neither company could manufacture such a tube without fear of being sued by the other.

The answer, of course, was for AT&T and RCA to join forces. An agreement was worked out on July 1, 1920, that allowed each company to manufacture the tube. AT&T also granted rights to RCA to establish and maintain one-way wireless transmitting stations and to use its telephone lines to send radio programs to the transmitter. With these stations David Sarnoff hoped to realize his old goal of selling "radio music boxes" for use in private homes.

RCA moved toward broadcasting at a slow pace because decisions had to be cleared through its parent company, General Electric. While RCA inched toward broadcasting, Sarnoff's goal was first achieved by a rival company called Westinghouse. Ironically, Westinghouse had been forced into broadcasting by the agreement between RCA and AT&T.

Westinghouse had been a competitor of RCA's parent company, GE, for years. Westinghouse had manufactured radio equipment for the American war effort. After World War I the company

President Warren G. Harding is sworn into office. Radio station KDKA broadcast Harding's victory on election day.

sought to establish its own international communications network. But Westinghouse quickly discovered that international two-way communication was jointly controlled by RCA and AT&T.

Shut off from two-way communications, Westinghouse concentrated on the undeveloped field of broadcasting. The company already had purchased exclusive rights to Armstrong's regeneration and superheterodyne patents.

The job of developing this market was given to Frank Conrad, an engineer who had radio experience. Conrad had been broadcasting piano and saxophone music from an amateur radio station set up behind his house. His broadcasts had become popular among local amateur operators. Westinghouse put Conrad in charge of building a radio station on the roof of its factory in Pittsburgh, Pennsylvania. The plan was simple: to hear broadcasts from the new station, people would buy radio sets manufactured by the company.

The Birth of Broadcasting

On November 2, 1920, station KDKA went on the air, broadcasting election returns for the 1920 presidential election. Those who owned radio sets went to bed that night knowing that Warren G. Harding had been elected president of the United States. A Westinghouse story released soon after the event described the historic broadcast. "Not only in Pittsburgh were the returns heard, but in many towns in Ohio, Pennsylvania and West Virginia the messages were heard with equal clearness. Letters are still being received from operators from many miles around thanking us for giving the returns so promptly."

Although KDKA was the first government-licensed station, it was not the first station to broadcast radio programs. Experimental broadcasting had been going on for over a decade. What was important about KDKA was the fact that it was the first time a major corporation had sponsored a radio station.

KDKA's broadcast was a huge success. Sales of its radio receivers skyrocketed. The station soon broadcast the first church service, the first prize fight, and other programs. Westinghouse quickly established other stations in Newark, New Jersey, and East Springfield, Massachusetts.

The success of KDKA spawned many companies that manufactured and sold radio receivers in violation of the patents. It also pushed RCA into action. Sarnoff saw his dream being realized by another company. The solution was again to join forces with the competition, as RCA had done months earlier with AT&T.

On March 21, 1921, an agreement was reached with Westinghouse. Westinghouse was given RCA stock and a portion of RCA's orders for radio parts. It also received the right to use RCA and AT&T patents to manufacture radio equipment for RCA.

In return, RCA gained access to the valuable Armstrong regeneration and superheterodyne patents controlled by Westinghouse. For the first time, one corporation, RCA, had legal access to all of the important patents that comprised the highest level of radio technology for radio transmitters and receivers. RCA and the radio industry were poised for dramatic growth in the decade that became known as the Roaring Twenties.

The success of KDKA sparked a revolution in the radio industry, as companies rushed to exploit the lucrative field of radio broadcasting. Within two years of the time that KDKA went on the air, 220 stations were started. Radio sets in homes had jumped from 50,000 sets to between 600,000 and 1 million. Millions of Americans gathered around the radio sets at night to listen to programs.

By virtue of his 1916 memo that predicted broadcast radio, David Sarnoff was hailed as a visionary. But radio broadcasting developed differently

A replica of the KDKA transmitter used to broadcast election results in 1920. KDKA's success sparked a revolution in the radio industry. Hundreds of radio stations vied for listeners, and sales of radio sets skyrocketed.

from how Sarnoff had envisioned it. In 1916 he had described radio as a cultural medium, similar to the public radio network of today. The cost of running the stations would be met by increasing the prices of the radio sets sold. But on August 28, 1922, station WEAF in New York broadcast an advertisement for apartment buildings, the first paid radio commercial.

The face of radio broadcasting was forever changed as a whole new profit area opened up—advertising. It solved the question of how radio stations could pay for themselves. Many businesses started their own radio stations to advertise their products. In 1923 WEAF announced that it would sell air time to any interested advertiser. Businesses suddenly had the opportunity to use the new advertising medium without the expense of setting up and maintaining a station of their own.

The presence of advertising cast a new light on the alliance between RCA and AT&T. AT&T's president, Sherman Gifford, soon realized that the 1920 agreement limited his company's profits in the radio industry. Gifford ordered AT&T to sell its RCA stock, and its members resigned from RCA's board of directors. Gifford also ordered AT&T's laboratories to develop a receiver that skirted RCA's patents. He decreed that RCA could no longer use AT&T's telephone lines for its remote and network broadcasts. He announced that AT&T's radio stations would aggressively promote toll broadcasting, or selling advertising to other companies. These steps put AT&T in direct competition with RCA and threatened RCA's future.

The bitter rivalry was halted in December 1923 when the Federal Trade Commission ruled that RCA, AT&T, and other companies participating in its agreements had created a monopoly on manufacturing and selling receiving sets. The ruling forced RCA and AT&T officials to work out a new agreement, which was completed in July 1926.

A KDKA broadcast session. Musical programs were among the favorites of listeners at home.

An Oregon family gathers around a radio in 1925. Farm families, often isolated from their neighbors, especially benefited from radio.

AT&T sold its WEAF radio station to RCA and closed its network of radio stations, a move that marked its withdrawal from broadcasting.

RCA established a self-supporting company that would create and broadcast radio programs over a number of stations linked together by telephone lines to form a network. The network was called the National Broadcasting Company (NBC). As part of the new agreement between RCA and AT&T, NBC agreed to pay one million dollars each year to use only AT&T telephone lines to link its radio stations.

With the creation of NBC, the modern age of radio networks began. A rival network, the Columbia Broadcasting System (CBS) was founded in 1929 by William S. Paley. NBC was divided into two semi-independent networks called the Red Network and the Blue Network. The Blue Network later became the American Broadcasting Company (ABC).

A network broadcast used both radio and telephone technology. The radio program originated in a particular radio studio, from which it was transmitted over telephone lines to the other stations in the network. Each station took the program off the telephone line and sent it through its transmitter, broadcasting it to all radio receivers tuned to that station's frequency. The network allowed people throughout the country to hear the broadcast simultaneously. The network was a remarkable addition to radio. People speaking in New York could be heard live in households across the country in California.

Radio Regulation

As with all industries, government and radio professionals soon realized that their industry needed regulations to provide for orderly development. As early as 1922 the federal government called together radio professionals for the first national radio conference. The conference determined that the government should have legal authority over commercial radio stations. It also determined that radio was a public utility and should be regulated in the public interest.

The industry accommodated the growing number of stations by adapting

An NBC broadcast featuring singer Ethel Waters. With the creation of NBC, the modern age of radio networks began.

the tuning technology pioneered by wireless engineers. When a radio station was started, it was assigned a particular frequency from which to broadcast its signal. Radio receivers were tuned to the station's frequency to receive its broadcast. A new station was also assigned a specified number of watts, or power, which limited the distance the broadcast could travel. This allowed stations far away from each other to occupy the same frequency without fear of overlapping.

Despite these measures the air be-came a jumble of radio signals as the number of stations grew during the 1920s. Many stations illegally boosted their power to send their signals farther and thus increased their advertising market. Other stations changed frequencies without permission. Amateur radio operators broadcast without regulation, further choking the airwaves. The result was terrible reception up and down the tuning dial.

In 1927 Congress passed the Radio Act, creating the Federal Radio Commission (FRC). The FRC was granted authority to establish and maintain regulations that brought order to the broadcasting industry. (The FRC was later renamed the Federal Communications Commission.)

Turning the Airwaves into Gold

In 1920 radio had been a novelty in American households. But by the end of the decade, radio was no longer primarily a method of two-way communication. A whole new industry, broadcasting, had been born. New technology had made radio receivers easy to use. Radio networks were linking the country as it had never been brought together before. As the decade changed, radio was about to enter what many call its golden age.

CHAPTER 6

Radio's Golden Age

It could be argued that radio's golden age began on October 19, 1929. On that day the stock market crashed, plunging the United States into an economic depression that lasted nearly a decade. During the depression's worst years, almost one of every four workers had no job. Factories reduced their output or shut down altogether because no one had any money to buy products. Homeless men called hobos wandered about the country. In many cities hungry people stood in lines for food.

Despite the hard times the radio industry remained healthy. In fact, the depression probably contributed to radio's success. While many movie houses and theaters closed down, radio prospered because it offered inexpensive entertainment. People could stay in their homes and listen to the news or be entertained by variety shows, children's programs, comedies, dramas, live music concerts, and sports events. Businesses and manufacturers quickly recognized this fact and continued to advertise their products on radio, which kept the industry healthy.

Radio was more than inexpensive entertainment. It was becoming a part

Radio entertained, comforted, and informed a nation badly hurt by the strains of the Great Depression. By this time, radio was on its way to becoming an important part of people's lives.

of people's lives. "Here was a medium of entertainment that was free . . ." wrote radio historian Irving Settel. "Thousands of families who had purchased much of their household equipment on credit gave up their vacuum cleaners, their cars, and their furniture, but kept up the payments on their radios. Radio had become a part of their lives with which they could not part."

Radio was also used to bring hope of better times to the American people. On March 4, 1933, millions of Americans gathered around their radio sets to hear their new president, Franklin Delano Roosevelt, deliver his inaugural address. He promised Americans a new economic and political program and assured them that they "had nothing to fear, but fear itself." Then on the evening of March 12, President Roosevelt again addressed the nation by radio. In a warm, conversational tone that evoked people chatting by the fireplace, Roosevelt talked about banking. He

told listeners about the steps he was taking to pull the country out of the depression. He reminded his audience that the nation's problems were as much their problems as they were his, and he called upon the people to work together.

Roosevelt obviously understood the power of radio, and his messages of hope helped start the nation on its way toward economic recovery. Although Roosevelt was not the first politician to use radio to spread his message, he was the first to use it so effectively. During his years as president Roosevelt held many fireside chats with America.

While Roosevelt and advertisers understood radio's power, perhaps no one yet understood that radio was changing America. The network broadcasts united the nation in ways it had never before been united. Radio brought the same programs to radios in rural America that were heard in the largest cities. "Radio's spellbinding voice was heard

During his fireside chats, President Franklin Roosevelt spread his message of hope. These radio broadcasts helped start the nation on its way toward economic recovery.

Ethel Barrymore's appearance in a radio play encouraged other movie stars to cross over into radio.

stage and movie actress Ethel Barrymore in a radio play, other movie stars crossed over into radio. Before long, radio stars began making movies, often with radio themes.

Daytime radio serials with continuing plots were often built around romantic themes. The serials were broadcast at a time when homemakers were doing household tasks and most sponsors were soap manufacturers. Thus, these programs were known as soap operas. Humorist James Thurber gave the recipe for a successful soap opera in a *New Yorker* magazine article: "Between thick slices of advertising spread twelve minutes of dialogue, add predicament, villainy, and female suffering in equal measure, throw in a dash of nobility, sprinkle with tears, season with organ music, cover with a rich announcer sauce, and serve five times a week."

There were hundreds of radio programs during the 1930s. Most of them have long since slipped from memory. But a handful of programs made permanent impressions on American culture and are remembered as classics.

The comedy show "Amos and Andy" joined the NBC radio network in 1929 under the sponsorship of Pepsodent toothpaste. The series revolved around the lives of two men, Amos Jones and Andy Brown, played respectively by Freeman Gosden and Charles Correll, and events at their taxicab company. The program became so popular, it is said, that President Roosevelt avoided interrupting the show with his fireside chats. The show also demonstrated how effectively radio could create images in the listener's mind. Amos and Andy were black characters, but the actors who played them were white. In more recent times "Amos and Andy" has been criti-

everywhere, and its influence was felt in every phase of life," wrote historian Settel. "New expressions were popularized, new names became nationally famous, and new modes of eating, dressing and thinking were almost hypnotically suggested by the voices from the box in the living room."

As a result of radio's influence, the distinct regional cultures that existed in America began to break down. A more homogeneous national character began to emerge.

Radio Favorites

Radio had drawn its early personalities from vaudeville, the variety show theaters in large and small towns. By the middle of the decade radio had created its own stars. After the appearance of

Comedian Fred Allen, pictured here, and Jack Benny boosted audience interest by engaging in a long-running, put-on feud. Each comedian chided the other on his own show.

money or your life," the robber demanded. After one of the longest silences in radio history, the robber demanded, "Well?" "I'm thinking it over," Benny replied.

Comedian Fred Allen had several radio shows and was famous for his biting wit and literate comedy. Allen and Jack Benny boosted audience interest in their shows by engaging in a long-running, put-on feud. Each comedian chided the other on his own show. When the feud reached the boiling point, the two men finally met on Jack Benny's show on March 14, 1937, supposedly to fight it out. The demand for studio audience tickets was so large that the program had to be moved to the ballroom of a New York hotel. Publicity shots for the broadcast show the two comedians reaching for each other's throats. The audience loved it. Radio survey figures show that only one of Roosevelt's many fireside chats drew higher ratings.

cized for using white actors and reinforcing stereotypes about African-Americans.

"Fibber McGee and Molly" was a radio comedy that starred Jim and Marian Jordan in the title roles. The running gag of their show occurred when Fibber McGee opened the door to the hall closet—despite Molly's warning. The audience was treated to a host of sound effects as an avalanche of junk came tumbling out.

Jack Benny established himself as one of radio's great comedians during this period. On his show he cultivated the reputation of being the stingiest man alive. He drove an old Maxwell car that scarcely ran and kept his money in an elaborate vault. On one show a robber stuck a gun in Benny's back. "Your

Invasion from Mars

The trust that people had come to place in radio was evident in one of its most famous dramatic broadcasts. On the night of October 30, 1938, a CBS announcer introduced Orson Welles's adaptation of H. G. Wells's science fiction book, *The War of the Worlds*. Music followed the introduction of the show. Suddenly the music was interrupted by the urgent voice of a different announcer: "Ladies and Gentlemen, we interrupt our program of dance music to bring you a special bulletin. At 20 minutes before 8 o'clock Central Time, Professor Farrell of Mt. Jennings Observatory, Chicago, reports observing several explosions of incandescent gas occurring at regular intervals on the planet Mars."

During the next hour and fifteen minutes, a series of news bulletins terrified listeners throughout the nation. These bulletins told of Martian invaders with deadly ray guns spreading death and destruction in New Jersey and New York. The next day's edition of the *New York Times* described the panic:

> The broadcast disrupted households, interrupted religious services, created traffic jams and clogged communications systems . . . at least a score of adults required medical treatment for shock and hysteria. In Newark, in a single block at Heddon Terrace and Hawthorne Avenue, more than twenty families rushed out of their houses with wet handkerchiefs and towels over their faces to flee from what they believed was to be a gas raid. Some families began moving household furniture. Throughout New York families left their homes, some to flee to near-by

parks. Thousands of persons called the police, newspapers and radio stations here and in other cities of the United States and Canada seeking advice on protective measures against the raids.

It was hours before the nation calmed down enough to realize that the broadcast was only a Halloween prank. Hundreds of complaints were received by CBS and the FCC. The FCC later issued a statement strongly discouraging further programs with faked news content. Panic aside, this incident dramatically illustrated the solid presence of radio in daily life.

The Development of FM Radio

Radio had become so popular, so necessary in homes and businesses that the next logical step seemed to be to give radios mobility. This is what engineers did when they developed radio re-

A 1938 radio dramatization of H.G. Wells's "War of the Worlds" panicked thousands of Americans who believed that an army from Mars had invaded New Jersey.

ceivers for passengers' automobiles and trucks. People were able to listen to their favorite radio programs while they were driving.

But car radios also highlighted a flaw in overall radio reception—the annoying buzz of noise known as static. Static was caused when static electricity in the atmosphere—sparks, or some types of motors—interfered with the AM radio signal. Radio engineers had wrestled with this problem for years. The problem was solved by radio genius Edwin Howard Armstrong, who had already given the industry regeneration and the superheterodyne.

Armstrong had studied the static problem for years and turned to frequency modulation (FM) in an attempt to solve it. He was not the only engineer to work with FM, but, in his usual manner, he challenged all of the conventional attitudes. This allowed him to make important breakthroughs.

Like amplitude modulation (AM), in which the amplitude or height of the wave is modulated or controlled, frequency modulation used a standard carrier wave. The carrier wave was combined with the irregular audio signal to produce the broadcast signal. Instead of modulating the amplitude of the wave, however, FM modulated the frequency of the wave.

Reducing Static

Armstrong's efforts to reduce static with frequency modulation met with failure until he discarded conventional thinking about bandwidth—the space a sound signal occupies when it is imprinted upon a carrier signal. Other engineers believed that the narrower the

bandwidth, the less chance for interference. That belief was correct for AM broadcasts. Armstrong discovered that FM waves could have a wider bandwidth.

The discovery forced him to design an entirely new radio system. First he passed the signal through a superheterodyne circuit, where it was turned into an intermediate frequency wave, just like an AM signal. Then he passed that wave through two completely new circuits he had invented. The first, which he called a limiter, removed any variations in the amplitude of the signal that it might have picked up in leaving the transmitter. Next, the wave passed through a discriminator, which changed the FM wave back into its original form. The wave then passed through an audio amplifier and emerged from a speaker as sound, just as AM signals did. Armstrong applied for five patents, which he received late in 1933.

Staticless Radio

On December 23, 1933, Armstrong invited his friend David Sarnoff of RCA to his laboratory to view a demonstration of staticless radio. Sarnoff heard a transmission that was free of static and much clearer than an AM signal. After this demonstration Sarnoff allowed Armstrong to put test equipment on top of RCA's headquarters at Radio City in New York. Sarnoff later recalled that he had witnessed not a demonstration, but a revolution in radio.

While Armstrong's FM work solved the problem of static over the airwaves, it created many problems for the industry. Despite the improved signal clarity, the industry was slow to embrace the

FREQUENCY MODULATION

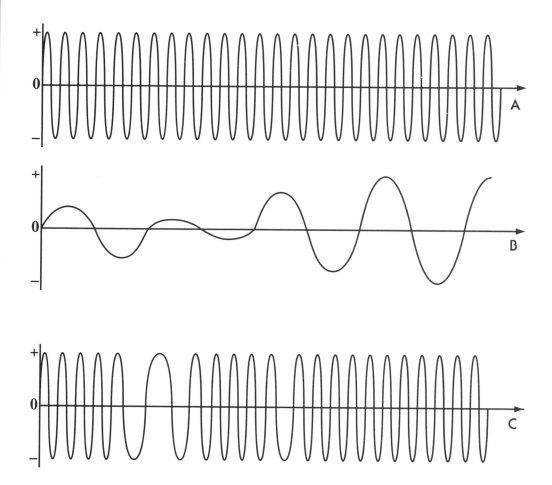

Like amplitude modulation, frequency modulation combines a constant carrier signal [A] with the irregular audio signal [B] produced by a microphone. The result is a broadcast signal [C] constant in amplitude but varied in frequency. Because the frequency of the signal changes, or modulates, the signal is known as a frequency modulation, or FM, signal.

The FM signal is less affected by interference than is the AM signal. This is because many things—static electricity, running motors, and stray sparks—cause changes in the amplitude of a broadcast signal. Since AM encodes sound waves as changes in amplitude, the sudden changes in the amplitude cause unwanted noises, such as crackles and pops, in the broadcast. Since FM encodes sound as changes in the frequency of the broadcast signal, changes in amplitude do not affect the sound of an FM broadcast. The result is a cleaner, crisper radio reception.

FM radio offered clear, static-free sound but it caught on slowly because of resistance from AM broadcast companies. Once it was introduced to the public, however, FM radio immediately took hold.

new technology. At RCA several circumstances made Sarnoff stall about giving Armstrong approval to develop FM for RCA. Twenty years earlier Sarnoff had enthusiastically witnessed Armstrong's regeneration and superheterodyne demonstrations. Those inventions had contributed to RCA's success with AM radio.

Now with interests to protect Sarnoff evaluated Armstrong's FM invention in economic terms. FM could make all other radio technology obsolete. The costs to change over from AM to FM broadcasting would be enormous. Sarnoff also did not think that the public would be willing to pay more money for an FM receiver. And Sarnoff had committed RCA's resources to develop technology that would send pictures as well as voices and music through the air. This new area in broadcasting was called television.

Sarnoff put RCA's future ahead of his long-term friendship with Armstrong. To make way for the new television equipment, he ordered Armstrong to remove his FM equipment from the top of Radio City.

Although he was hurt by Sarnoff's order, Armstrong pressed on alone. In 1936 he petitioned the FCC to grant him a license for an experimental FM station. He selected a site in Alpine, New Jersey, and began construction of his station in 1938, financing it himself.

On July 28, 1939, station W2XMN, the world's first FM station, went on the air. That same month General Electric began selling the first FM radio receivers.

Armstrong's development of FM opened the door to many technological developments in radio. It was soon discovered that FM signals operating on the same wavelength did not interfere with each other as AM signals did. The FM receiver simply picked up the stronger signals. This meant that FM stations could be placed closer together than AM stations could, which would allow more radio stations to be built. When the FCC assigned specific FM frequencies on the radio wave spectrum, applications for broadcast licenses came pouring in.

The FM signal had other advantages over AM. Unlike AM signals, which had to be relayed over telephone lines, FM signals could be relayed through the air. This meant that an FM radio network would not have to rely on telephone wires, the way AM networks relied on telephone lines to link their many stations together.

In a fitting irony, FM also became part of television technology when engineers discovered that FM was the best way to transmit the audio portion of television. In 1939 RCA began to broadcast television programs from its towers atop Radio City. The television audience was small because sets were expensive and the picture quality was poor. But, as he had in 1916, Sarnoff had looked into the future of communications and realized that television was the wave of the future.

The two technologies, FM and television, were poised for dramatic commercial growth as the 1930s came to an end. But just as the development of voice radio had been interrupted by World War I, a new war brought FM and television development to a halt.

Radio and World War II

Throughout most of the 1930s Americans had heard disturbing radio reports about the rise to power in Germany of Adolf Hitler and the Nazi party. On September 1, 1939, Germany invaded Poland, touching off World War II. With Italy as its ally, Germany quickly conquered much of Europe. Soon, only Britain stood against Germany and Italy, known as the Axis powers. In 1940 Britain's prime minister Winston Churchill broadcast a grim promise across occupied Europe: "We shall never surrender."

For two years the United States remained neutral in the war. On December 7, 1941, Japanese airplanes attacked the naval base at Pearl Harbor, Hawaii. The next day President Roosevelt addressed the nation by radio in a voice filled with determination. "Yesterday, December 7, 1941, a date that will live in infamy," he began, "the United States of America was suddenly and deliberately attacked by naval and air forces of the

Britain's prime minister Winston Churchill (left) left no doubt about his nation's resolve during World War II when he announced over radio, "We shall never surrender."

Empire of Japan . . . ." Roosevelt requested Congress to declare a state of war between the United States and Japan. Germany and Italy, which were allies of Japan, soon declared war on the United States.

America's armed forces had quietly been preparing for war for years, adapting the two-way radio technology that was developed for civilian use. Improvements in both transmitters and receivers had made two-way voice radio commonplace in daily life. Police cars, emergency vehicles, taxicabs, and delivery vehicles relied on two-way radio to reduce response times to calls. Because FM reception was superior to AM reception in two-way communication, most two-way systems used FM to transmit signals.

Largely through the efforts of Edwin Howard Armstrong, FM was also adopted for two-way communications systems developed by the army and navy. The transmitters and receivers

that went to war in 1941 were much smaller than their World War I counterparts, and they had greater range. Tanks, trucks, ships, and other equipment were furnished with FM radio transmitters and receivers. Portable units called walkie-talkies were carried by soldiers.

FM gave the Allied forces, an alliance of nations led by the United States, Britain, and France, an advantage over their enemy. FM signals were less susceptible to static and, therefore, more reliable than the AM signals used in German radios. Better communication allowed the Allied forces to move troops quicker, which won battles and saved lives.

Broadcast radio also played a significant role in the war. Because a radio broadcast reached millions of people, radio became an important tool for both sides. On the Allied side, the Armed Forces Radio Network was formed to support and entertain Allied

A taxi driver receives information for his next pick-up. Police cars, emergency vehicles, taxicabs, and delivery vehicles came to rely on two-way radio for quick response to calls.

Radio played an important role in World War II. Radio operators in the chart room of the aircraft carrier USS Lexington *keep information flowing during a strike on the Gilbert and Marshall islands (left). Soldiers relay information by radio from a foxhole in Kiska, Alaska (below).*

troops. America's top entertainers performed on the network. By war's end the network covered the globe with more than 800 stations.

The Axis powers also used broadcast radio. In Germany a woman known to Allied troops as Axis Sally broadcast largely false information about Nazi victories and Allied losses to demoralize Allied troops. In the Pacific another woman known as Tokyo Rose made similar broadcasts. Often Allied naval forces who tuned in heard false reports that the ships they were listening from had been sunk by Japanese planes.

Radar, a detection device that used radio waves, also figured prominently in the Allied war effort. Radar, which stands for **ra**dio **d**etecting **a**nd **r**anging, was developed by the U.S. Navy in the

Radar operators track enemy aircraft before notifying fighter pilots to intercept the planes.

1920s. The concept behind radar was fairly simple. A beam of radio waves was sent out by a transmitter at the speed of light. When the beam struck a solid object, it was reflected back toward the transmitter. A steady stream of reflected radio beams created an electronic spot on a screen that represented a plane or ship. The beams also revealed how far away the object was and in what direction it was traveling.

Radar helped the British Royal Air Force detect German bombers in 1942 and foil Nazi attempts to destroy Britain with mass bombing. Radar also helped Allied destroyers detect the presence of German submarines before they could attack.

After four bitter years the Allied forces prevailed. They claimed victory in Europe in May 1945. On September 2, 1945, Japan formally surrendered to the Allied forces and the war ended.

A few months later, Edwin Howard Armstrong gave a demonstration based on radar research he had conducted during the war. On January 10, 1946, he and army engineers bounced a radio signal off the moon and back to earth. The signal traveled more than a quarter of a million miles to the moon and back in about two and a half seconds. Forty-five years after the first signal spanned the Atlantic, radio had reached out and touched the moon. It would remain for future generations of radio engineers to reach for the stars.

From Tubes to Transistors

The outbreak of World War II had delayed the widespread introduction of both television and FM broadcasting. With the war over, the industry picked up where it left off. Both television and FM radio threatened the established domain of network AM radio. But the networks, led by RCA, embraced television and continued to stall the development of FM radio. The golden age of radio came to an end. It would take an amazing new invention called the transistor to help revive the broadcast radio industry.

Radio Versus Television

Sarnoff's decision in 1936 to remove Armstrong's FM broadcasting equipment from the roof of Radio City and replace it with RCA's own television equipment had changed the direction of the industry. RCA was the largest, most powerful radio company in America, and the rest of the industry usually fell in step behind it. To Sarnoff FM was only an improvement on existing AM radio technology, but television was the wave of the future. In the preface of *The First 25 Years of RCA*, published just before the war ended, Sarnoff wrote, "We find the Allies headed for victory. Peace will find the world on the threshold of television . . . all radio will be changed." Elsewhere in its pages, the book promised that RCA would bring "the glories of television" to the public.

NBC, the broadcast network of RCA, resumed its television broadcasts shortly after the war ended. At first the

Radio, once the center of many family gatherings, quickly lost ground to television. But the radio industry held on thanks to a new invention called the transistor.

network served only viewers between Boston, Massachusetts, and Washington, D.C. Other networks also began broadcasting television programs. Sales of television sets increased dramatically. Americans' entertainment habits began to change. While radio maintained much of its daytime audience, its evening audience began to erode. Families gathered around television sets at night to watch comedian Milton Berle, whose nickname became "Mr. Television," as they had once gathered around their radios to listen to Jack Benny.

By 1951 television programs were being broadcast from coast to coast and radio was losing many of its star performers and much of its audience to television. It was clear that the age of television had arrived and that the radio industry was starting to decline. A bruising fight over FM had not helped matters at all.

Troubled FM

Eager to promote television and wary of FM's encroachment on AM radio, the networks had used the FCC to cripple the fledgling FM industry. The tool of FM's near destruction was television. Like radio, television required frequency ranges for its audio and visual signals. To prevent chaos on the wide spectrum of radio waves, these frequencies had to be assigned by the FCC. AM radio already occupied a frequency range of 500-1600 kilohertz (kHz) on the mid-frequency range of the radio spectrum. FM radio occupied a higher frequency range on the spectrum, 42-50 megahertz (mHz).

Television could function at any frequency range. But the broadcast networks, which supported AM and television, saw an opportunity to strangle FM radio by forcing it to move elsewhere on the spectrum. The vacated frequen-

By 1951 the age of television had arrived. Families gathered around television sets to watch programs broadcast from coast to coast.

cies would be assigned to carry television's audio and visual signals. The networks knew that such a move would have little effect on the quality of television broadcasts, but the move would make all FM radio equipment obsolete. Existing FM transmitters and receivers could be tuned only to the 42-50 mHz FM frequencies.

To advance this plan, false rumors were circulated that FM at 42-50 mHz was bothered by sunspots—periodic dark spots on the sun that affected radio transmissions. If FM were moved to higher frequencies on the spectrum, according to the rumor, there would be less interference caused by sunspots. The rumors ignored the point that if FM radio was affected by sunspots at its existing frequency range, so would the audio signal of television, which was transmitted by FM!

FM Development Hindered

A commission of broadcasters studied the problem and suggested leaving FM where it was on the spectrum. Nevertheless, on January 15, 1945, the FCC announced that FM was being moved from 42-50 mHz to 88-108 mHz on the radio spectrum to "preserve the quality of its service." The news for FM radio could not have been worse. The relocation made obsolete nearly a half million radio receivers and transmitting equipment at fifty FM stations. A new generation of FM equipment that could be tuned to the newly assigned frequencies had to be built, and this would probably take years.

Further actions approved by the FCC hurt FM radio's development even more. The FCC allowed AM broadcasters to duplicate their programs on FM frequencies. Few people would buy an FM receiver to hear a program they could already pick up on their AM receivers. By duplicating programming, AM stations could serve FM listeners without additional programming costs. The AM stations were also able to provide low advertising rates for AM and FM packages and this helped AM retain its hold on the existing advertising market. This hold made it difficult for FM stations to sell advertising. FM stations needed advertising revenues to finance their operation.

Using a plan developed by CBS vice president Paul Kesten, the FCC placed a third limitation on FM broadcasting known as the single market concept. The FCC limited the power output of FM stations so that their signal would not pass beyond a single city or, in advertising terms, a single market. The networks convinced FCC officials that the plan would allow more FM stations to exist, because their signals would not overlap. But Kesten knew what the real effect of his single market plan would be. Confined to a single market, FM stations would have such small audiences that they would have to struggle to sell advertising. Without advertising sales to help them grow, FM stations would remain small operations that would not threaten AM radio.

FM Stations' Power Declines

The FCC action hurt FM radio in another way too. When the FCC limited FM's power output, in effect, it raised the cost of FM broadcasting. Because

FM signals traveled through the air between relay towers, FM avoided the more expensive telephone wire transmission required for AM broadcasts. By reducing power output, the FCC reduced the distance the FM signal could travel between towers. To transmit their signals FM broadcasters would have to erect many more towers, which would in turn raise the cost of doing business.

The FCC's single market plan greatly reduced the power of all FM stations including Edwin Howard Armstrong's own FM station in Alpine, New Jersey. In addition, it curtailed the growth of a new FM network called the Yankee Network, which soon would have competed against the established AM networks.

Armstrong Versus RCA

Edwin Howard Armstrong grew increasingly angry over the way the industry had blocked the advancement of FM. He was angry that RCA and other television manufacturers were using FM in television sets without paying him a licensing fee. His anger was directed at RCA and, in particular, his old friend David Sarnoff.

On July 22, 1948, Armstrong sued RCA and NBC for infringing on his five basic FM patents. The odds seemed against Armstrong, for he was a lone inventor battling the largest corporation in the industry. But for Armstrong the principle was as important as the money he had been denied by what he believed was the illegal use of his patents.

For RCA in particular the suit threatened the company's future as Sarnoff envisioned it. If Armstrong won, RCA would be denied the right to manufacture radio and television sets that used FM. The suit dragged on for years, as RCA and NBC used every legal means at their disposal to prevent the case from going to trial.

The long legal struggle took its toll on Armstrong. His single-minded pursuit of the lawsuit caused a separation from his wife. His health declined. The fortune that he had made from licensing his inventions was consumed by legal expenses. At a low point, the despondent Armstrong told friends that "they [RCA and NBC] will stall this thing until I am broke or dead."

Armstrong proved to be his own prophet. As America's most brilliant radio engineer, he had invented much of the technology upon which RCA had been built. But the long battle with RCA had left Armstrong a broken man.

A bitter lawsuit against RCA and NBC demoralized Edwin Howard Armstrong. He committed suicide in 1954.

Radio newsrooms, such as this one in the NBC studio, provided remote broadcasting and on-the-spot news and traffic coverage, making radio the first place to turn for news and traffic reports.

On January 31, 1954, he composed a letter of apology to his wife, Marian. Then he stepped out of the window of his thirteenth-floor apartment and plunged to his death.

Marian Armstrong continued her husband's legal fight against RCA and NBC. A settlement awarding her $1,050,000 was eventually worked out. Armstrong had also sued other companies for violating his patents. One by one, settlements were negotiated in Marian Armstrong's favor.

The successful settlements seemed to justify Armstrong's twenty-year devotion to FM and his stubborn defense of his patents. The real justification, however, came not in these court settlements, but in the widespread adoption of FM broadcasting that lay in the future.

The Transistor Age

It became obvious after a few years that radio was not being completely replaced by television, as the automobile had replaced the horse and buggy. Several factors combined to adapt the radio industry to fit the changing times.

Radio networks and independent stations alike began to recognize the limits of television and concentrated on delivering services that television could not. They realized that television cameras could not be moved easily from place to place. With television confined to studios, radio executives emphasized remote broadcasting and on-the-spot news and traffic coverage, making radio the first place to turn to for news and traffic reports.

After World War II, engineers William Shockley, Walter Brattain and John Bardeen (left to right) unveiled a new device that could replace the inefficient vacuum tube. Their invention was called a transistor.

But the radio industry needed a boost if it was to prosper in a world dominated by television. In 1948, three Bell Laboratories engineers, Walter Brattain, William Shockley, and John Bardeen, unveiled a small device called a transistor. Small and compact, it looked nothing like a radio vacuum tube. There was no glass, no grid or filament, no moving parts. It was nearly solid and did not even heat up. Yet, astoundingly, it functioned exactly like a vacuum tube.

The three men had started their research soon after the end of World War II. Their mission was to replace the vacuum tube. Although far superior to the

vacuum tubes in early radios, postwar tubes were still fragile and prone to frequent burnout. Vacuum tubes had to be heated in order to stimulate the movement of electrons, which made the tubes work. This required far more power than the power of the radio signal that the tubes pulled from the air. Thus, vacuum tubes were inefficient.

The engineers drew upon advancements in solid-state physics, a science that studied the structure and behavior of atoms in solid objects. Scientists had known for decades that some materials, such as metals, were conductors of electricity. Other materials such as glass were nonconductors of electricity, also known as insulators. They came to understand that, in conductors, atoms have one or more electrons that move freely from atom to atom, creating the current. On the other hand, in nonconductors, the electrons do not move freely, which blocks the flow of current.

Scientists also came to understand that some materials share properties of conductors and nonconductors. They conduct electricity much better than nonconductors, but not as well as conductors do. These materials are called semiconductors.

The Bell engineers hoped to use this knowledge to develop a way to stimulate and control the movement of electrons in solid objects. They were true pioneers, like Marconi, Fleming, De Forest, Armstrong and others, using crude

Transistors, like vacuum tubes, transmit, receive, and amplify radio signals, but they are smaller, less expensive, and more efficient.

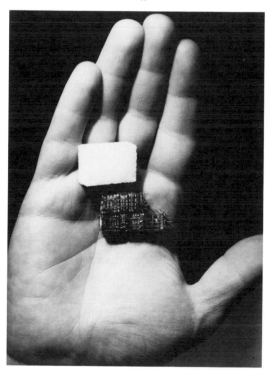

materials they had on hand that had the properties they desired.

Their first working transistor was constructed by wrapping gold foil around a plastic knife edge. They slit the foil with a razor blade to make two closely spaced lines of foil. This was pressed against a block of a crystal called germanium, a semiconductor, that had an electrical connection at its base. A small, positive electric voltage was applied to one line of foil (called the emitter) and a large negative voltage to the other (called the collector). When electric current was fed into the germanium at the emitter, it flowed not to the contact point on the base but to the collector and added to the current flowing through the collector. The crude device amplified the current by a factor of fifty.

The engineers knew what had happened even if they could not see it. With a small amount of current, the transistor had controlled a much larger amount of current and increased its power many times.

From this crude beginning engineers were able to develop transistors that transmitted, received, and amplified radio signals, just like vacuum tubes. The transistor, however, was much smaller than a vacuum tube. It was inexpensive to make. It was far more efficient and lasted much longer than a vacuum tube.

Although it would be several years before transistors were incorporated into radios, the transistor made an important contribution to the radio industry's survival. When transistor radios did come on the market, they were cheaper and more portable than vacuum tube radios. Although the old console, or cabinet-style, radios that stood

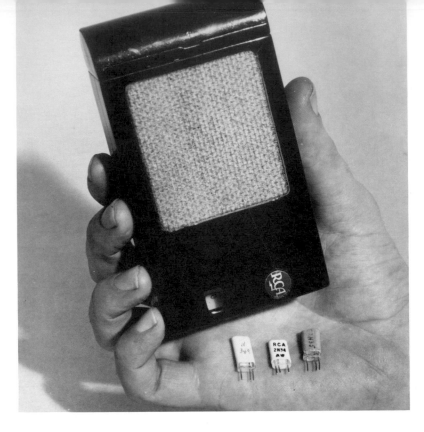

Mass marketed portable radios were made possible by the invention of the transistor.

in America's living rooms were steadily replaced with television sets, Americans did not quit buying radios. They moved newer, smaller radios to kitchens, bedrooms, even back to the workshop, where radio enthusiasts had first tinkered with primitive sets at the turn of the century.

The invention of the transistor allowed radios to become truly portable for the first time. Although portable vacuum tube radios had been marketed, they were large and bulky. They required so much energy to heat the tubes that the batteries ran down quickly.

But these limitations vanished in October 1954 when the first mass marketed portable transistor radios were shipped to stores by Industrial Development Engineering Associates of Indianapolis, Indiana. This radio was tiny by all previous standards. It measured only 3 by 5 by 1.25 inches in size and could

be held in the palm of a hand. It contained no tubes, functioning with four transistors powered by a 22.5 volt B battery.

Transistor radios were a sensation. They were carried on picnics, to the beach, on boating and camping trips—virtually everywhere. No matter where they were, Americans could be entertained or stay informed about the day's events, something that television could not yet do for them.

The introduction of transistor radios coincided with a new form of youth-oriented music that swept the country in the mid-1950s—rock and roll. A new radio format evolved—records played by a disc jockey (DJ). Unlike radio announcers of earlier days, the disc jockey did more than introduce the records. The DJ was a personality. By engaging in lively banter over the air, and sometimes talking to listeners on the telephone, the DJ became part of the program. Young listeners tuned in to hear the DJ almost as much as the music.

Stereo and FM

After being stalled for two decades, FM broadcasting began to grow in the 1950s. From the time when Armstrong had first introduced it in 1939, FM broadcasting drew praise for its high fidelity, or ability to reproduce the original sound. But Sarnoff and other radio executives had determined that radio and television audiences did not really care about sound quality. They continued to use AM signals in radio, and inferior amplifying equipment in FM television sets. In a sense the radio executives were right: audiences could hardly miss what they did not know about.

In the 1950s, however, high fidelity reached American homes in the form of stereo recordings and stereo record players, or hi-fi's. Stereo recordings were made by placing two microphones in different parts of the studio while music was being recorded. What each microphone picked up was preserved in separate channels. This separation was preserved in the pressing of the vinyl record. When the record was played on a stereo system containing two speakers, the music originally preserved in each channel was reproduced in a separate speaker. As technology improved, many instrumental or voice performances could be separately recorded and mixed into the two channels of a stereo system.

Interest in stereo recordings led to listener interest in stereo broadcasting. At last FM had something to offer that AM and television could not offer. Be-

In the mid-1950s, along with rock and roll, came a new radio format—records played by a disc jockey (DJ). DJ's became as much a part of the radio program as the music.

cause FM had a wider band than AM, it could pick up the very high- and very low-frequency sounds heard in stereo recordings, which AM could not.

The stereo signal was created through multiplexing. Multiplexing is the process of combining several audio signals on the same carrier wave. These signals can be broadcast to differently tuned receivers at the same time. To create a stereo signal, a broadcast wave was created and the two channels of the stereo recording were imprinted on the broadcast wave in separate audio signals. In the home, the FM receiver picked up the broadcast wave, separated the two audio signals from it, and broadcast them in separate speakers.

The FCC licensed the first stereo

From the high-fidelity stereo system, or hi-fi, of the 1950s (left) to the portable Walkman and headphones of the 1990s (right), broadcast radio continues to entertain and inform.

FM station in 1961. Through the 1960s and '70s, the number of stations broadcasting stereo FM signals grew steadily. Today FM broadcasting is a flourishing industry, and FM stations actually outnumber AM stations in the United States. In 1992 at least 6,189 radio stations broadcasted in FM, while at least 4,089 broadcasted signals in AM.

Here to Stay

The fear that television would replace radio as radio had once replaced wireless telegraphy has long since disappeared. Today radios come in all sizes and prices. Listeners can hear the news or their favorite programs over elaborate home stereo systems costing thousands of dollars. Or, they can hear the same programs while wearing inexpensive headphones that have AM and FM receivers built into them.

Broadcast radio and television exist side by side. Radio executives continue developing new formats to meet changing life-styles. By adjusting either their AM or FM receivers, listeners can hear a wide variety of radio formats: network news, talk shows, foreign language programs, classical music, progressive rock, rap, oldies, jazz, easy listening, and country, to name a few. In one form or another, broadcast radio continues to be a daily part of our lives.

Radio in the Space Age

On October 4, 1957, the world was stunned by sensational news: the Soviet Union had successfully sent an unmanned satellite into orbit in outer space. The incredible event became a milestone in history, symbolizing the beginning of a new era in our technological abilities. The world had entered the Space Age.

While broadcast radio continues to inform and entertain, radio in its many other forms has made contributions, large and small, to life in the Space Age. Radio signals have been used to increase our understanding of the universe and even for running many household appliances.

Five years after the first satellite was sent into orbit, communications literally joined the Space Age. Throughout the 1950s and '60s an increasing number of long distance telephone calls was transmitted on radio waves instead of through telephone wires. The radio signals were relayed by tall towers spaced about thirty miles apart.

On July 10, 1962, AT&T took communications into space by launching *Telstar*, the world's first communications satellite, into orbit. *Telstar*'s complex transistors received long distance calls that had been turned into radio waves and relayed them to distant cities where the signals were fed back into telephone wires. *Telstar* could receive and relay up to 240 telephone conversations at one time.

Today dozens of communications satellites orbit the earth, relaying radio signals that carry radio broadcasts, com-

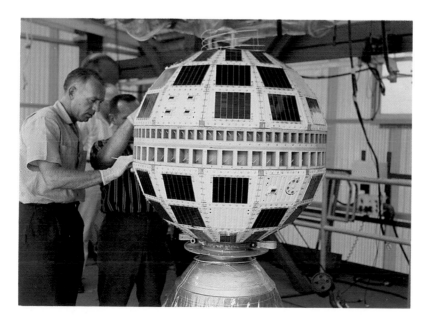

Telstar, *the world's first communications satellite, expanded the global telephone network. Worldwide communications now rely on dozens of satellites that process information via radio waves.*

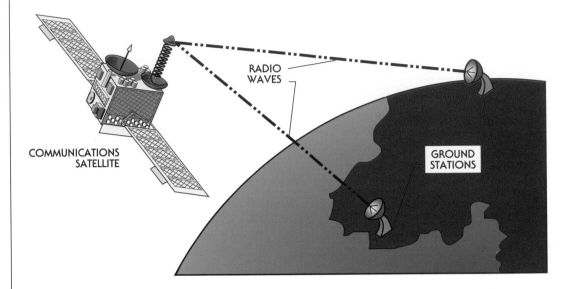

COMMUNICATIONS SATELLITES

RADIO WAVES

COMMUNICATIONS SATELLITE

GROUND STATIONS

Communications satellites make it possible to relay radio signals all the way around the world. The radio waves are beamed to a satellite from a transmitting station on the earth. The satellite receives these signals and relays them to an on-board amplifier. The amplifier strengthens the signals and retransmits them to another earth station. The second ground station then amplifies the signals and broadcasts them nearby.

puter data, television sound and pictures, and telephone conversations across continents and oceans. The satellites orbit at the same speed as the earth revolves; thus, they are always stationed over the same spot on the earth below, serving as relay towers in space.

From Transistors to Microchips

Space Age technology has also created a new generation of transistors called microchips. The microchips make the transistors used in the original portable radios and *Telstar* look as bulky and primitive as an old vacuum tube.

Microchips are constructed from chemically altered semiconductor materials. The result is microscopic circuits that conduct electric currents. In effect, this technology shrinks a transistor to microscopic size and places thousands of them in a single chip.

Microchips are inexpensive to make. They are considered to be up to ten thousand times more reliable than the transistors of the early 1960s. Because they are so tiny, thousands of them can be packed into a small space, making them very powerful.

Radio and other communications equipment that use microchips are smaller and far more powerful than equipment constructed with first-generation transistors. For example, while *Telstar* could handle only 240 telephone messages at a time, modern communications satellites can handle 36,000 messages at a time.

Exploring Space and the Universe

Radio signals have played an important role in developing America's space program and increasing scientists' knowledge about the universe, too. When astronauts were first sent into space in the early 1960s, ground controllers relied on a vast, global network of radio equipment to track spacecraft as they orbited

Tiny microchips pack far more power than transistors ever could.

Communications satellites, such as the Advanced Communications Technology Satellite, orbit the earth. They carry radio broadcasts, computer data, television sound and pictures, and telephone conversations across continents and oceans.

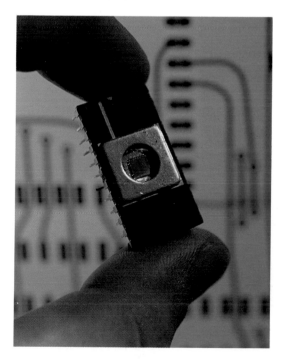

the earth. Astronauts used voice radio to communicate with controllers on the ground. Throughout each flight streams of data collected by a spacecraft's onboard computers were relayed on radio signals back to earth. In the future, men and women may live on permanent space stations and use radio signals to maintain communication with earth.

Although spacecraft carrying astronauts have traveled only as far as the moon, purely mechanical space probes have traveled into distant parts of the solar system. As these probes traveled through space, they have sent back to earth radio signals containing data that scientists study for clues about the nature and origins of the solar system.

Space probes are not the only

source of radio signals reaching earth from space. Stars are also reaching out to earth with radio waves. From observations originally made in the 1930s, scientists have discovered that many stars emit radio waves. Adapting the concept of the telescope, scientists have constructed huge radio telescopes that collect radio waves. These telescopes paint data pictures, rather than visual pictures, of distant stars. Scientists study data from radio telescopes to learn about stars and to search for clues to the origin of the universe.

Two-Way Communication

Space Age technology has also created two-way communication devices that existed only in science fiction a generation ago. For example, in the 1960s tele-

Radio signals transmit information from space. The Magellan space probe (above) begins its long journey to the planet Venus. It will send information back to earth through radio signals. Huge radio telescopes (left) collect radio waves from stars. The telescopes paint data pictures, which scientists study to learn more about the universe.

vision series "Star Trek," the crew of the *Enterprise* opened wallet-size "communicators" to talk to their shipmates. When the series was created, such compact personal communication devices were only a dream. But Space Age technology has made steady progress toward such compact communicators, creating numerous forms of reliable two-way communication that are inexpensive and easy to use. Today's two-way communication equipment would indeed astound people who paid telegraphers to relay personal messages in code across cumbersome wireless systems.

Citizens band (CB) radio became popular in America during the 1970s, when the FCC expanded to forty the number of channels it had originally designated for two-way communication between private citizens.

The operation of CB equipment can be mastered in a short time. A CB unit is both a transmitter and a receiver. Each of the forty channels has a differ-

Citizens band (CB) radio became popular in America during the 1970s. While the craze faded by the mid-1980s, truckers, farmers, and others still use CB radios to communicate.

ent frequency range. CB users contact each other on channel 19. Once contact is established, the parties agree to switch to a different channel to continue their conversation, leaving channel 19 open again. CB owners can easily change channels and listen in on conversations between other users. This means that CB radio communication is public, which partly accounts for CB's immense popularity.

In the late 1970s citizens band radio became a national craze. Millions of units were sold to enthusiasts who installed stationary units in their homes and mobile units in their cars and trucks. CB users adopted humorous names, known as handles, and sometimes developed whole new personalities to go with their names. CB enthusiasts formed clubs and sponsored picnics and charity events. A CB language soon evolved, and dictionaries were even published. Movies and songs built around CB themes entertained the entire nation. Amid all of the fun, CB users exchanged information about weather and road conditions as they drove the nation's roads and highways. They notified authorities of emergencies, traffic accidents, and road hazards.

The craze faded by the mid-1980s. Truckers, farmers, and others still use CB radios to communicate.

Cellular Radio

About the time that CB radio reached its peak and began to fade as a national craze, a new form of personal two-way communication called cellular radio was coming of age. Cellular radio combined radio and telephone technology to dramatically widen the scope of two-

The cellular radio, which uses both radio waves and telephone technology, enables users to speak to almost anyone in the world who has a telephone.

way communication. While CB users generally can talk only to other CB owners, the cellular radio user can speak to almost anyone in the world who has a telephone. Because cellular radio uses both radio waves and telephone technology, people often use the term cellular telephone when referring to the equipment.

Cellular radio replaced an earlier form of mobile telephone service that relied on a single, high-powered transmitter to service an entire metropolitan area. There were few communication channels available, and service was poor and costly.

On April 9, 1981, the FCC approved the concept of cellular mobile radio telephone service. On December 8, 1982, the FCC announced a construction permit for Advanced Mobile Phone Service, Inc. (AMPS), to provide cellular service to the Buffalo, New York, area. The FCC issued AMPS permits for Pittsburgh and Chicago at about the same time. Other permits followed.

Cellular radio divides a metropolitan area into a series of clusters. Each cluster has seven cells that range in diameter from about twelve to twenty-four miles. The cells are hexagon shaped because that shape best allows all areas of a city to be covered without gaps. In each cell a low-powered radio transmitter is linked to a central office called a mobile telephone switching office (MTSO). The MTSO is linked by telephone lines to the nation's telephone system.

Each mobile cellular unit has a unique telephone number. The mobile phone monitors a special radio channel called a set-up channel. An incoming call from a standard telephone or another mobile phone comes into the MTSO, which signals the correct phone by sending a message to all of its cells over the set-up channels. This is called a page. The correct phone picks up the signal and rings, and the owner answers. As an automobile passes from one cell to another, the MTSO automatically switches the signal to the next cell. This procedure is known as a handoff.

To make a call the user dials the number just as with a regular telephone. The signal is picked up by the transmitter in the cell and relayed to the MTSO. Then the signal is fed into the telephone system, where it reaches the desired party.

In remote areas not serviced by an MTSO, cellular radio can achieve its links by using communications satellites. Thus, it is possible to contact anyone owning a telephone from remote places hundreds of miles from a standard telephone.

Personal cellular radio units that operate on batteries are carried by many businesspeople who must leave their offices or cars behind. They easily fit in a pocket or briefcase. In 1991 sales of pocket cellular radios topped one million units, more than ten times the number sold just four years earlier. The

A businessman uses a personal cellular radio unit, also called a cellular telephone.

world's lightest cellular unit was introduced in 1992, weighing under half a pound. It cost $945.

One-Way Communication

Not all personal radio communication needs to be two way. Many applications of one-way radio communication serve us daily. Pagers are devices that use radio waves to signal doctors, delivery and service people, and other individuals, usually by way of a beeping sound. The individual who has been paged uses the nearest telephone to call the message center, office, or home, or finds the caller's phone number displayed on the pager. Motorists tell their garage doors to open by pushing a button and sending a radio signal that orders a motor to raise the door.

One-way transmitters are even attached to wild animals so that scientists can monitor them and learn more about their populations and habits. Transmitters dropped in the mountains can signal the outbreak of forest fires or other disasters. Children send radio signals to make model airplanes fly or model cars race down the sidewalk.

New Technology in the Twenty-First Century

As the world approaches a new century and a new millennium, scientists continue to develop new technology using radio and radio waves. This new technology promises to enrich our lives and serve our information needs.

New technology is already in the experimental stage. For example, radio transmitters and receivers of the future may rely on pulse code modulation (PCM) rather than frequency or amplitude modulation. PCM adapts the digital binary language used by computers. In this language, voices, letters, musical notes, and even pictures are converted electronically to combinations of 1s and 0s. In transmission, a pulse of radio energy represents a 1; a pause represents a 0. The radio receiver reads the pulses and pauses and converts them back into the original voice, letter, musical note, or picture. Because it has only two elements—a 1 or a 0—a pulse signal is simpler than AM or FM signals and, therefore, less subject to interference. This makes digital audio quality superior to that of both AM and FM. PCM represents the wave of the future in two-way radio and telephone communication. To avoid the tremendous cost of replacing old two-way communication systems with PCM all at once, communications companies will probably incorporate PCM equipment over a period of time.

In broadcast radio this pulse technology is usually called digital audio broadcasting (DAB). DAB offers exciting new opportunities in the field of broadcasting. Because of its audio superiority to AM and FM, DAB is the best method for sending radio signals by satellite. In the near future DAB technology will probably be used to create satellite radio services similar to cable or satellite television. DAB radio receivers will be able to take the signals relayed by satellite from radio stations hundreds of miles away. Thus, listeners in California may be able to hear stations from New York or Florida in addition to the California stations they already listen to.

When it becomes a reality, DAB and satellite radio will again revolutionize broadcast radio. But radio history seems to be repeating itself. Just as AM broadcasters stalled FM decades ago,

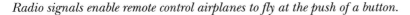

Radio signals enable remote control airplanes to fly at the push of a button.

The teleconference, using two-way radio communication devices, has become an important part of business communication, overcoming time and distance barriers.

both AM and FM broadcasters are currently fighting the development of DAB. Through their opposition to DAB, these broadcasters hope to protect their heavy investments in AM and FM technology. Some industry experts predict that DAB will reach listeners by the end of the 1990s. Even those who are resisting its development acknowledge that DAB will delight listeners in the twenty-first century.

The need for more and faster communication continues to grow almost daily. Radio is an important component in the complex communications equipment that sends enormous amounts of data through the air. In the next century radio science will increasingly be integrated with telephone, television, and computer technologies to build exciting new communications and data processing devices.

From the time that Marconi first developed his wireless telegraph to send messages, two-way radio communication has been an important part of our daily lives. Throughout the years and in many forms, two-way radio communication devices have steadily become more compact, more reliable, and less expensive. New two-way communication devices will be developed that surpass the pocket-size cellular radio units of today. Just as every household of today has a telephone, in the twenty-first century, every individual may have a personal communication device.

Throughout the history of radio science engineers have reconsidered the scientific knowledge and technology around them and made marvelous new discoveries. Step by step, radio advanced from mere theories to crude devices to the sophisticated Space Age equipment that is part of our everyday lives. In today's technology are locked the secrets to great radio discoveries in the twenty-first century. By reconsidering what they already know, scientists will discover new ways to improve or adapt our existing technology. They may even discover new types of radio waves in the spectrum and develop marvelous new technology to harness them.

Glossary

▪▪

amplitude: The highest or deepest point of a radio wave.

amplitude modulation (AM): A method of broadcasting radio signals in which the amplitude of the radio wave is modulated, or controlled.

Branly coherer: An early radio device for detecting radio signals.

cellular radio: A form of personal two-way radio communication that combines radio and telephone technology. Also called cellular telephone.

cycle: One repetition of an electromagnetic wave.

diode: A glass vacuum tube used to receive radio signals.

Edison effect: The one-way movement of electrons in a vacuum tube when a negative charge is applied to the filament and a positive charge is applied to a nearby metal plate. First observed by Thomas Edison in 1883, this was the foundation for the development of the diode and triode.

electromagnetic wave: A wave created by the relationship between magnetism and electricity. Often called a radio wave.

electron: The negatively charged portion of an atom. The movement of electrons creates an electric current.

frequency: The number of cycles a radio wave travels in one second.

frequency modulation (FM): A method of broadcasting radio signals in which the frequency of the radio wave is modulated, or controlled.

microchip: A device that contains thousands of tiny transistors used in modern communications equipment.

Morse code: A coded alphabet devised by Samuel F. B. Morse for sending messages over telegraph wires. Morse code was used to transmit messages in the early days of radio, before equipment that transmitted and received voices was invented.

oscillator: An early device for generating radio waves.

patent: Exclusive rights to an invention, granted in writing by governments.

radio: The science of transmitting voices, music, and other sounds through the air with electromagnetic or radio waves. A receiver of radio waves is often referred to as a radio.

receiver: Device that receives radio signals sent through the air by a transmitter and turns them back into sound.

regeneration: The process of feeding an amplified radio signal back into the circuit where it is amplified again. This happens thousands of times each second, giving an audio signal its volume.

semiconductor: Material that conducts electricity better than a nonconductor, but not as well as a conductor. Silicon is a semiconductor used in radio components.

signal: A simple or complex radio wave sent by a transmitter to be picked up by a receiver.

spark-gap generator: An early device for generating and transmitting radio signals.

superheterodyne: The first modern radio receiver. The device simplified tuning a receiver to two knobs, one controlling frequency, the other volume.

transistor: A solid-state device made with semiconductors and used in both radio transmitters and receivers. The transistor replaced vacuum tubes in radio transmitters and receivers.

transmitter: Device that sends radio signals through the air to receivers.

triode: A glass vacuum tube invented in 1906 by Lee De Forest that amplified radio signals. Also known as an audion.

vacuum tube: Early radio component used to transmit or receive radio signals.

wave length: The distance from the peak of one wave to the peak of the next wave.

wireless telegraphy: The forerunner of voice radio. Used Morse code to transmit telegraph messages with electromagnetic waves instead of wires. The first commercial wireless communication system was established by Guglielmo Marconi.

For Further Reading

Doug DeMaw, *First Steps in Radio*. Newington,
CT: American Radio Relay League, 1985.

Susan Gilmore, *What Goes On at a Radio Station?*
Minneapolis: Carolrhoda Books, 1984.

Irwin Math, *Morse, Marconi and You:
Understanding and Building Telegraph, Telephone
and Radio Sets.* New York: Charles Scribner's
Sons, 1979.

Ross R. Olney and Ross D. Olney, *The Amazing
Transistor, Key to the Computer Age.* New York:
Atheneum, 1986.

Works Consulted

Isaac Asimov, *How Did We Find Out About Microwaves?* New York: Walker, 1989.

Len Buckwalter, *The ABCs of Citizens Band Radio.* New York: Howard W. Sams, 1975.

Len Buckwalter, *Beginner's Guide to Ham Radio.* Garden City, NY: Doubleday, 1978.

Douglas Coe, *Marconi: Pioneer of Radio.* New York: Julian Messner, 1943, 1961.

Orrin E. Dunlap Jr., *Communications in Space: From Marconi to Man on the Moon.* New York: Harper & Row, 1970.

Tom Lewis, *Empire of the Air: The Men Who Made Radio.* New York: Edward Burlingame Books, 1991.

John R. Pierce and A. Michael Noll, *Signals, The Science of Telecommunications.* New York: Scientific American Library, 1990.

Stan Prentiss, *Introducing Cellular Communications: The New Mobile Telephone System.* Blue Ridge Summit, PA: Tab Books, 1984.

Hans Queisser, *The Conquest of the Microchip.* Cambridge, MA: Harvard University Press, 1988.

Irving Settel, *A Pictorial History of Radio.* New York: Bonanza Books, 1960.

John W. Stokes, *70 Years of Radio Tubes and Valves.* Vestal, NY: The Vestal Press, 1982.

Index

About the Author

Roger Barr is a writer and publisher who lives in St. Paul, Minnesota. He has written widely on business, historical, and cultural subjects for various commercial and trade magazines. He is the author of *The Vietnam War* and *The Importance of Richard M. Nixon* for Lucent Books and the novel *The Treasure Hunt* published by Medallion Press.

Picture Credits

j   4-94
621.384
Barr, Roger

Radios: wireless sound

WITHDRAWN